CHINESE
IN STEPS

STUDENT BOOK 2
步步高中文2

George X Zhang
Linda M Li
Lik Suen

华语教学出版社 · 伦敦
Sinolingua · London

Every effort has been made to trace all copyright holders, but if any have been inadvertently overlooked, the publisher will be pleased to make the necessary arrangements at the first opportunity.

Chinese in Steps Series
Chinese in Steps (Student Book 2)
By George X Zhang, Linda M Li, Lik Suen

Editor: Zhang Le, Du Ranran
Cover Design: China-i

This new version, first published and Copyright © 2012 by Sinolingua London Ltd. is published under permission from Cypress Book Co., (UK) Ltd. The original version of Chinese in Steps Volume 2 (ISBN 9781845700041) was published by Cypress Book Co., (UK) Ltd. in 2006.

Unit 13, Park Royal Metro Centre
Britannia Way
London NW10 7PA
Tel: +44(0)2089519305
Fax: +44(0)2084530709
E-mail: editor@cypressbooks.com
Website: www.sinolingua.com.cn

Distributed by Cypress Book Co., (UK) Ltd.
Tel: +44(0)2084530687
Fax: +44(0)2084530709
E-mail: sales@cypressbooks.com
Website: www.cypressbooks.com

Printed in the People's Republic of China

ISBN 978-1-907838-11-8

About This Series

Chinese in Steps is a series of textbooks designed for English-speaking adults who learn Chinese either as part of their degree study at university, or simply as part of their professional or self-development programme for practical purposes. While aiming to deliver an effective result and an enriching experience of learning Chinese language, it has also taken into consideration the needs of those who seek externally validated qualifications.

Chinese in Steps differs from many other textbooks in its approach to language teaching, and in its conscious effort to make use of adult learners' own rich experiences in learning Chinese. Its approach is based upon how English-speaking adults learning Chinese and aims to deliver language teaching with an integrated method of communicative approach, contrastive analysis and cultural awareness.

Chinese in Steps aims to develop learners' productive communicative competence by focusing on key generic speech patterns and making listening and speaking the core activities of each lesson. The book also aims to develop learners' reading and writing skills with a systematic introduction to relevant knowledge backed up with practice based upon cognitive research, as reading skill is crucial for adult learners to acquire if they expect to use and understand Chinese effectively. The layout of the book is designed to make the contents easy to access and follow. Necessary grammar explanations are given where necessary, but grammatical jargon is kept to a minimum.

Chinese in Steps currently consists of four student's books and one teacher's book. The structure of the student's books, two at Beginner's and two at Lower Intermediate levels, is similar, and these two levels are designed to cover most key speech patterns, fundamental grammatical knowledge, 880 frequently used characters, and over 2000 words. By completing the four books, learners should have covered enough ground to be able to cope with many everyday life needs in a Chinese speaking environment and to reach a sound basic B1 level as an independent learner, as proposed by this series with regard to the Common European Framework of Reference. The four books in the series are interconnected and progressive, with the first two books at Beginner's level aiming to achieve a basic A2 level. The coming teacher's book will provide practical guide for users of Books 1 and 2. Book 3 continues to build and develop the linguistic and cultural competences of learners while Book 4 consolidates and further cultivates such competences of learners by engaging them in various real tasks in everyday life situations.

Chinese in Steps can be used for university Chinese language programmes or non-credit bearing part-time Chinese language courses for adult learners. In terms of the level attainable, the completion of the first two books will cover enough knowledge and skills to prepare for high GCSE, Intermediate Level in the Asset Language scheme and the New HSK Levels 4/5. All the books in the first two stages are accompanied with audio CDs.

Chinese is often perceived as a difficult language in Europe, especially Chinese characters, but its difficulty lies primarily in the fact that it is so different from European languages. It is important to have a ***relaxed*** and **confident** attitude to the learning of the Chinese language. **Chinese in Steps** in many ways endeavours to help learners achieve confidence by gradual introduction to the characteristics of Chinese language as adults learn better and more effectively with a good understanding of what they are doing.

Language skill is acquired over a long period of time and with frequent practice. Learning and revising **bit by bit** and practising **constantly** and **frequently** are keys to success for adult learners who usually find it difficult to devote much time to study. So before you start to learn Chinese, it is important to remain relaxed and confident during the learning process, to enjoy the experience of entering a different linguistic world, and to study and practise gradually and frequently what you learn.

Preface

We are very happy to be able to present this brand new edition of *Chinese in Steps* by Sinolingua London. This is the first new edition of the series since it was first published in 2005 by Cypress Book Co. We are also most delighted that due to the dedication and support from our users, this series was a recent recipient of the Award for Outstanding International Chinese Language Teaching Materials at the Fifth Confucius Institute Conference in December 2010.

Over the last few years, there has been an apparent and rapid growth in the number of people learning Chinese in the UK and around the world. This increase has not only led to a growing demand for quality textbooks, but has also called for the creation of learning and teaching materials that are able to meet the needs and requirements of a variety of students. Whilst we are confident that the content of our series effectively meets such needs, we still adhere to the principle that there is always further room to excel in our future work. We believe that the underlying principles that have guided its compilation and production are sound, based on a thorough understanding of both the needs of our users and how to best meet these needs. This understanding has been constantly enhanced by constructive feedback from our users, to whom we are most grateful. We have tried to incorporate into this latest edition as much feedback as possible so as to make the series even more user-friendly.

There have been some noticeable changes between this and the previous edition. First, real life photos are used in this edition, and we sincerely hope our users like them as it was one of the requests received in user feedback. Second, the number of Chinese characters in each of the first five lessons has increased from 20 to 22, thus bringing them in line with the rest of the book and the subsequent three books. Third, while the Pinyin that accompanies the speech patterns in each lesson has been retained, it is now placed underneath the Chinese sentences so it is less of a distraction for users. Some additional changes include the use of colours and indicators to make the important sections more visual, which was also a suggestion from our users. Besides these changes, the first two books of the series are now accompanied by a Teacher's Book, which we hope will be a useful guide filled with practical tips on using this textbook series.

We feel very fortunate and extremely grateful that so many users of this series, both teachers and students alike, have taken the time and trouble to provide us with their invaluable feedback. What you see in this book is very much the result of this feedback, and we would like to take this opportunity to thank all of our users for their care, consideration and support over all these years. We also sincerely hope that our users will find the changes in this new edition helpful, and will continue to provide their feedback and suggestions for this series.

Finally, we would like to thank Sinolingua London, a specialist publisher of Chinese teaching materials, and Cypress Book Co., the major distributor of this series, for their unremitting efforts and support in the publication of this new edition. Thanks must also go to all of our colleagues whose work made this new edition possible, especially Managing Director of Sinolingua London, Ms Ru Jing, and editors Ms Zhang Le and Du Ranran.

George X Zhang
Linda M Li
July 2011

语法术语简略表　Abbreviations of Grammatical Terms

adj	adjective
adv	adverb
comp	complement
conj	conjunction
id	idiomatic expression
int	interjection
l.w	location word
m.v	modal verb
m.w	measure word
n	noun
num	number
o	object
pt	particle
p.n	proper noun
pron	pronoun
prep	preposition
q.w	question word
s	subject
t.w	time word
v	verb
v-c	verb-complement
v-o	verb-object

☻ Chinese characters noted with * are usually not used on their own, but as a component of a word.

目录 Contents

预备课
Warm-up Lesson

Learning objectives

This is a revision of Book One. It covers the essential speech patterns and vocabulary taught in Book One. It is also a warm-up lesson to prepare you for Book Two.

对话 1 Dialogue One

王京： 小李，你好！这是我的中国朋友高明。

她是东方学院的学生。

李东： 你好！我是伦敦大学的学生，中文名字叫李东。

高明： 你好！

李东： 高明，你是中国什么地方人？

高明： 叫我小高吧。我是北京人。

李东： 好。我有个朋友谢红也是北京人，

也是东方学院的学生。

高明：是吗？我不认识她。她学什么专业？

李东：她学商业。

王京：小李，我们今天有个晚会，你来吗？

李东：我很想去，可是我今天很忙。

王京：你天天都很忙！今天是小高的生日。

李东：是吗？小高，生日快乐！

高明：谢谢。

王京：你们饿不饿？我们一起去吃饭，好吗？

李东：吃什么？吃三明治？

王京：今天是小高的生日，我们去吃中国饭吧。

李东、高明：好。我们走。

对话2 Dialogue Two

李东：小高，你喜欢打网球吗？

高明：喜欢。

李东：我们星期六一起去打网球，好不好？

高明：星期六我很忙。星期天怎么样？

李东：星期天我想回家看我爸爸、妈妈。星期一晚上怎么样？

高明：我不喜欢晚上打球。

李东：那你晚上都做什么？

高明：我晚上看电视、上网、做作业……。你呢？

李东：夏天我踢足球，冬天我打网球。

高明：你不做作业吗?

李东：做，我早上做。我们的作业很少。

高明：这个星期天你回家，我们下个星期天去打网球，好不好?

李东：好! 下个星期天见。

高明：下个星期天见。

Learning tip:

那 then, in that case
下个星期天 next Sunday

阅读 Reading

中国和英国

中国是一个大国，地大人多。英国比中国小，英国的人口 (population) 也比中国少多了。冬天，中国的北方很冷，北京就比伦敦冷很多，可是南方 (south) 有的地方和英国差不多 (about the same)。夏天，中国比英国热，英国的夏天天气很好，不冷不热。中国的春天比英国暖和，英国的春天和中国的秋天差不多，有一点儿冷。中国夏天雨多，冬天雪多。英国很少下雪，春夏秋冬都常常下雨。

中国人喜欢打羽毛球，英国人喜欢踢足球。中国人喜欢吃米饭 (plain rice)，英国人喜欢吃炒饭。中国人喜欢喝白酒和啤酒，英国人喜欢喝红酒和啤酒。中国人喜欢和朋友在家 (at home) 喝酒，英国人喜欢去酒吧 (pub) 喝酒。中国人常常吃红烧肉，英国人常常吃烤牛肉。中国人喜欢喝绿茶 (green tea)，英国人喜欢喝红茶 (black tea)。中国骑自行车的人多，英国开车的人多。

可是，中国和英国的青年人 (young people) 都喜欢吃美国 (USA) 快餐 (fast food)、看美国电影 (film)。

练习 Exercises

填空 Fill in the Blanks

Complete the following sentences by filling in the blanks with the appropriate words from the list below.

月　几　杯　吃　喝　坐　热　天天　还是　不　没　号

1) 我们要三 ⬜ 牛奶。

2) 我 ⬜ 晚上都看电视。

3) 北京夏天比伦敦 ⬜ 。

4) 你家有 ⬜ 口人？我家有五口人。

5) 你喜欢吃中国饭 ⬜ 英国饭？

6) 我今天很忙，你忙 ⬜ 忙？

7) 我 ⬜ 有姐姐，可是有一个妹妹。

8) 今天是十 ⬜ 六 ⬜ ，星期二 。

9) 她明天 ⬜ 火车去伦敦看她男朋友。

10) 我爸爸喜欢 ⬜ 中国饭， ⬜ 中国茶。

组句 Arrange the words in the correct order to make sentences.

E.g. 茶 两 要 中国 杯 他们 ——→ 他们要两杯中国茶。

1) 都(2) 我们(1) 英国人(4) 是(3)

_____

2) 今天(2) 还书(7) 他们(1) 图书馆(6) 坐(3) 去(5) 地铁(4)

_____

3) 小姐(2) 王(2) 打(5) 喜欢(4) 很(3) 网球(6)

_____

4) 老师(8) 中文(3) 是(5) 我们(1) 人(7) 北京(6) 的(2)

_____

5) 比(3) 冷(5) 冬天(2) 北京(1) 伦敦(4)

_____

6) 写(4) 他(1) 天天(2) 汉字(5) 晚上(3)

_____

7) 会(4) 烤鸭(6) 我(1) 做(5) 不(3) 妈妈(2) 可是(7) 会(8) 做红烧肉(9)

_____

8) 应该(4) 不(3) 英国人(1) 应(2) 外语(6) 学(5) ？(7)

_____

9) 女朋友(2) 的(3) 我(1) 比(5) 我(6) 胖(9) 的(7) 猫(4) 狗(8)

_____

10) 生日(6) 是(2) 明天(1) 我(3) 的(5) 哥哥(4)

_____

提问 Use question words to ask questions about the underlined parts of the following sentences.

1) 她叫<u>李小英</u> _____

2) <u>王红</u>是伦敦人。 _____

3) 他们都是<u>中国</u>人。 _____

4) <u>明</u>天是王京的生日。 _____

5) 我妹妹今年<u>八</u>岁。 _____

6) 下个星期天是<u>二十三</u>号。 _____

7) 我今年<u>十九</u>岁。 _____

8) 今天星期<u>四</u>。 _____

9) 我女朋友想去<u>北京</u>学汉语。 _____

10) 我爸爸天天<u>开车</u>去上班。 _____

翻译 Translation

Say the following sentences in Chinese first, and then write them out in characters.

1) What is your surname? My surname is Wang.

2) What is his nationality? He is Chinese.

3) What is the date today? February 19, 2012. It is my boyfriend's birthday.

4) He watches TV every evening.

5) I can speak a little Chinese, what about you?

6) Do you have any English books?

7) There are a lot of students at this university.

8) My brother is 5 years younger than I am, but he is taller than I am.

9) How will you get to the university library today? I shall go by bus.

10) My elder brother is a doctor; his girlfriend is a lawyer.

写作 Writing

Write a passage of around 150 characters about yourself or someone you know/like/fancy, using as many speech patterns and as much vocabulary as you can.

11

第十一课　　大英图书馆在哪儿？

Learning objectives
Ask for information on the location of something/someone
Give directions on how to find a place/person/thing
Talk about the position/location of something/someone

生词 New Words

请	qǐng	v	please; invite
问	wèn	v	ask (a question)
在	zài	v/prep	be at/in/on; at/in/on
旁边	pángbiān	n/l.w	side　　旁 side　边 side, edge
北边	běibian	n/l.w	north
东北边	dōngběibian	n/l.w	northeast
南面	nánmiàn	n/l.w	south　　南 south　面 side, face
西南面	xīnánmiàn	n/l.w	southwest　西 west
前头	qiántou	n/l.w	front　　前 front　头 tóu end; head
后面	hòumiàn	n/l.w	behind　　后 behind
左面	zuǒmiàn	n/l.w	left side　左 left
右面	yòumiàn	n/l.w	right side　右 right
中间	zhōngjiān	n/l.w	in the middle of　　间* between
外面	wàimiàn	n/l.w	outside
里面	lǐmiàn	n/l.w	inside　　里 inside
对面	duìmiàn	n/l.w	opposite side
银行	yínháng	n	bank　　银 silver　行 shop; firm
公园	gōngyuán	n	park　　园 garden
火车站	huǒchēzhàn	n	train station 站 station
大使馆	dàshǐguǎn	n	embassy 大使 ambassador 使 messenger
书店	shūdiàn	n	bookstore
张	Zhāng	n	Zhang (a surname)
国王十字	Guówáng Shízì	n	King's Cross (place name)
亚非学院	Yàfēi Xuéyuàn	p.n	School of Oriental and African Studies (SOAS) 亚* Asia (abbr.) 非* Africa (abbr.)
大英图书馆	Dàyīng Túshūguǎn	p.n	the British Library

句型 Speech Patterns

S	Adv	在	Place
张 先 生 Zhāng xiānsheng		在 zài	哪儿? nǎr?
张 先 生 Zhāng xiānsheng		在 zài	家。 jiā.
张 先 生 Zhāng xiānsheng	不 bú	在。 zài.	

在 precedes a place word to indicate the location of the subject. Please note that 是 is not needed in this structure. Negative and question forms follow the usual patterns.

A	在	B	(的)	LW
商店 Shāngdiàn	在 zài	车站 chēzhàn	的 de	东边。 dōngbiān.
大使馆 Dàshǐguǎn	在 zài	公园 gōngyuán	的 de	旁边。 pángbiān.
我家 Wǒ jiā	在 zài	商店 shāngdiàn	的 de	对面。 duìmiàn.

One can indicate the location of A in relation to B by following the speech pattern A + 在 + B (的) + LW. 的 is often omitted in spoken Chinese.

A (的)	LW	是	B
我 Wǒ	旁边 pángbiān	是 shì	我大哥。 wǒ dàgē.
我家 Wǒ jiā	后面 hòumian	是 shì	商店。 shāngdiàn.
银行 Yínháng	东边 dōngbiān	是 shì	一个图书馆。 yí gè túshūguǎn.

One can indicate the location of B in relation to A by following the speech pattern A + LW + 是 + B, which implies that the location is usually solely occupied by B itself.

A (的)	LW	有	B
商店 Shāngdiàn	对面 duìmiàn	有 yǒu	一个银行。 yí gè yínháng.
大学 Dàxué	旁边 pángbiān	有 yǒu	一个公园儿。 yí gè gōngyuánr.
火车站 Huǒchēzhàn	外面 wàimiàn	有 yǒu	很多人。 hěn duō rén.

One can indicate the location of B in relation to A by following the speech pattern A + LW + 有 + B. It is similar to "there is" in English.

补充词汇 Additional Vocabulary

网吧	wǎngbā	Internet bar	健身房	jiànshēnfáng	gym
厕所	cèsuǒ	toilet/WC	游泳池	yóuyǒngchí	swimming pool
电梯	diàntī	lift	电影院	diànyǐngyuàn	cinema
餐厅	cāntīng	dinning hall	花店	huādiàn	flower shop
学校	xuéxiào	school, college	快餐店	kuàicāndiàn	fast food shop
邮局	yóujú	post office	饭店	fàndiàn	restaurant; hotel

对话1 Dialogue One

高明：您好，张老师在吗?

李贵：他不在，他今天在大英图书馆看书。

高明：请问，大英图书馆在哪儿?

李贵：在火车站的旁边儿①。

高明：哪个火车站?

李贵：国王十字火车站。

高明：国王十字火车站在哪儿?

李贵：在亚非学院的东北②边。

高明：谢谢。对不起，哪面是东? 哪面是西?

李贵：你左面③是东，右面是西。

高明：谢谢。再见!

对话2 Dialogue Two

小王：大明，中国大使馆在哪儿?

小李：在亚非学院的的西南面。

小王：大使馆南面是一个大公园，对吧?

小李：不对。公园在大使馆的北边。

小王：大使馆外面有没有公共汽车站?

小李：有。大使馆对面有一个银行，车站就在银行前头。

小王：有没有地铁站?

小李：也有。地铁站在大使馆和公园的中间。

小王：谢谢。我明天想去大使馆，还想去书店。

小李：大使馆后面就有一个书店。

小王：里面有中文书吗?

小李：有。

语法注释 Grammar Notes

① **在火车站的旁边儿** — 儿 is added to some words in spoken Chinese, especially by people living in and around Beijing, to form a retroflex final marked by "r". However, it is not pronounced as an independent syllable. To add 儿 to a word can sometimes change its meaning or function, therefore do not add 儿 to words until you understand how to use it properly yourself.

② **Directions in Chinese** — Unlike in English, Chinese begins with the east and goes clockwise from there when speaking about the four directions. If it refers to directions in between these four directions, Chinese start with either east or west. Thus, southeast and southwest are 东南 or 西南, while northeast and northwest are 东北 and 西北 in Chinese, respectively！

③ **Location words** — Most location words can be formed with the suffixes 边, 面 and 头：

里边，里面，里头	外边，外面，外头
上边，上面，上头	下边，下面，下头
前边，前面，前头	后边，后面，后头

These location words are formed with the suffixes 边 and 面：

左边，左面	右边，右面	东边，东面
南边，南面	西边，西面	北边，北面

The following location words only have one form：

旁边，对面，中间

文化知识 Cultural Note

中国人和方位 Directions in Chinese Culture

Chinese culture attaches a positive value to the direction of south, which is also referred to as yang, signifying light, masculinity and strength. Long ago, Chinese farmers noticed that it was from the south that the most sunlight came. Most houses in China are built facing south, though nowadays in big cities houses and buildings are constrained by the street layouts and thus can be built facing any direction. It is interesting that the magnetic compass, a Chinese invention, is called 指南针 (zhǐnánzhēn, literally meaning south pointing needle) in Chinese.

练习 Exercises

口语练习 Speaking Practice

1. Working in pairs, talk about the position of each person or object in the pictures.

2. Working in pairs, take turns telling each other the position of each of the following objects, then re-arrange them and describe their new positions, see if your partner can work out their new positions.

3. Working in pairs, situate each of the following institutions in a numbered space of your choosing, and then describe its location. Number 5 and number 6 have been already assigned as 图书馆 and 大使馆, respectively.

⑤ 图书馆　商店　商学院　火车站　医院　银行　⑥ 大使馆

听力练习 Listening Practice

Listen to the short dialogues and circle the correct answer in each group, accordingly.

1)　a. 在前面　　　　b. 在左面　　　　c. 在右面

2)　a. 你旁边　　　　b. 你前面　　　　c. 你后面

3)　a. 银行西边　　　b. 图书馆东边　　c. 银行东边

4)　a. 公园的东面　　b. 公园的西面　　c. 公园的对面

5)　a. 王老师　　　　b. 李老师　　　　c. 女老师

6)　a. 有地铁　　　　b. 有汽车　　　　c. 有火车

7)　a. 在家　　　　　b. 在学院　　　　c. 在汽车里

8)　a. 骑车去　　　　b. 开车去　　　　c. 坐车去

语法练习 Grammar Practice

1. Multiple choice.

1)　王老师在 _____ 吗?

　　a. 家　　　　b. 哪儿　　　　c. 在不在

2) 图书馆的 _____ 有一家烤鸭店。

    a. 中间   b. 对面   c. 里头

3) 李太太在李先生 _____ 旁边儿。

    a. 前   b. 的   c. 右

4) 我家的后面 _____ 一个图书馆和两个商店。

    a. 有   b. 在   c. 是

5) 王小明天天 _____ 学校的图书馆里面看书。

    a. 是   b. 有   c. 在

6) 法国在英国的 _____ 。

    a. 西面   b. 东南面   c. 西南面

2. Re-write the following sentences by swapping the subjects. The first sentence has been done as an example.

1) <u>中国商店</u>在<u>学校</u>东面。 ⟶ 学校在中国商店西面。

2) 医院在公园的后边。

_____

3) 大使馆的左边是一个银行。

_____

4) 商学院不在大英图书馆北边。

_____

5) 王小明在我的左边，他太太在我的右边。

_____

6) 日本在中国的东北边儿。

_____

认字识词 Words with Known Characters

Figure out the English meanings of each of the words below and write them in the spaces provided.

外国 _____   国外 _____

上车 _____   下车 _____

下班 _____   酒馆 _____

茶馆 _____   饭馆 _____

南非 _____   东南亚 _____

天使 _____   外星人 _____

翻译练习 Translation

Say the following sentences in Chinese first, and then write them out in characters.

1) Is the library to the south of your home? No, it is to the north of my home.
2) The train station is opposite the bank.
3) There are a couple of shops outside our college.
4) The bookstore is between the library and the bank.
5) The Chinese Embassy is beside the park.
6) Mr Li is in the car outside.

阅读 Reading

伦敦大学亚非学院

亚非学院是伦敦大学的一个学院。学院不大，可是很有名 (famous)。学院有一个很大的图书馆，里面有很多图书，有英文的、中文的、还有日文的等等 (etc.)。天天都有很多学生和老师去图书馆借 (borrow) 书、还书、看书。

亚非学院在大英图书馆的西南面，大英博物馆 (museum) 的西北面。学院的东北面有三个中国饭馆儿，那儿的中国饭很好吃，也不贵，学生们都喜欢去那儿吃饭。学院的东边是一个小公园，西边是一个很大的书店。书店旁边有一个酒吧。很多学生和老师星期五晚上都去那儿喝酒。

Please answer the following questions based on the information in the above text.

1) What has been said about SOAS in the first paragraph?

2) Where is SOAS? What is there to the east of SOAS?

3) Why do many students go to Chinese restaurants northeast of SOAS?

4) What is there to the west of SOAS and what is beside it?

5) What do a lot of students and teachers do on Friday evenings?

汉字知识 Chinese Characters

偏旁 Radicals

The semantic associations of three radicals are given in the table below. Can you work out and write their related characters according to the pinyin provided?

女 (女, 女) woman	tā	hǎo	jiě	mèi	mā
口 (口) mouth	nǎ	pí	jiào	hē	chī
日 (日, 日) sun	zuó	xīng	chūn	wǎn	míng

汉字笔顺 Stroke Order

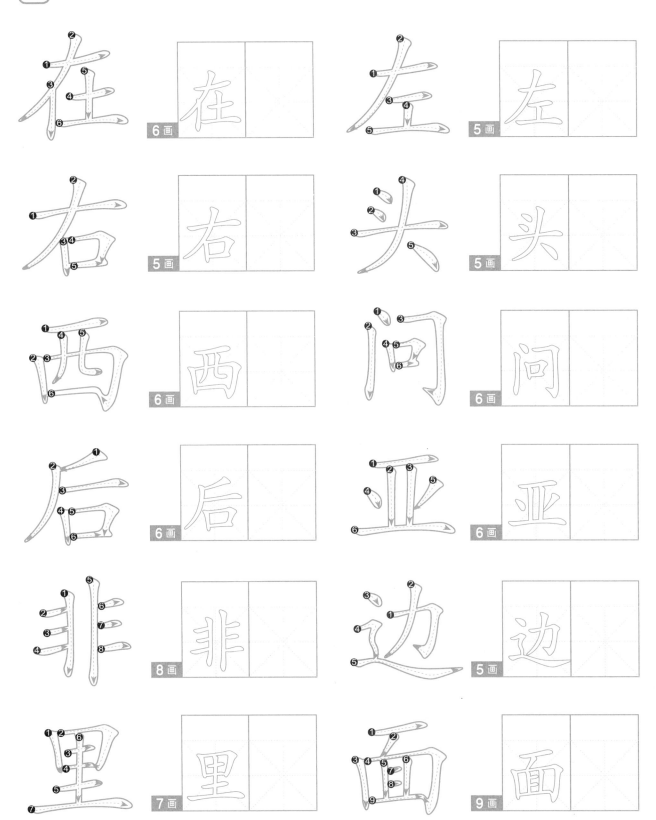

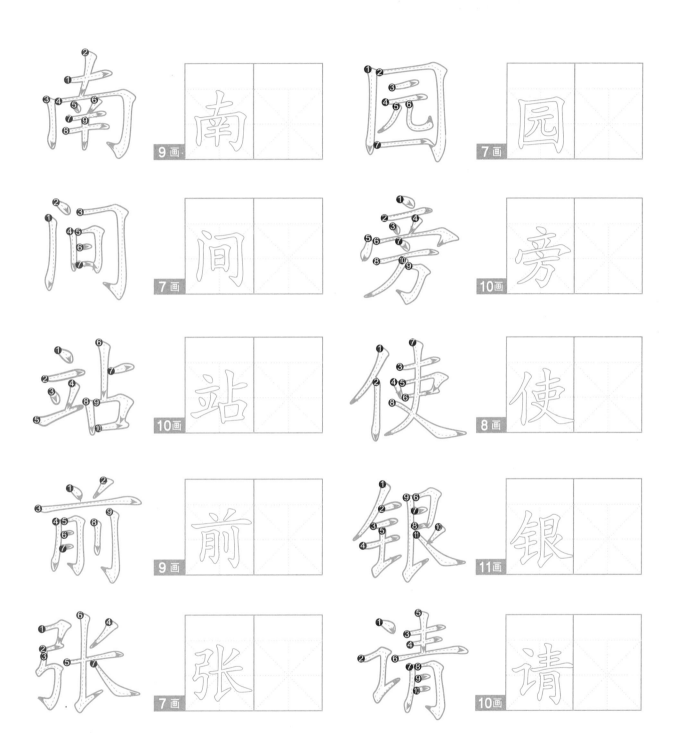

9画 南

7画 园

7画 间

10画 旁

10画 站

8画 使

9画 前

11画 银

7画 张

10画 请

12

第十二课   矿泉水多少钱一瓶？

Learning objectives

To learn how to ask about prices
To learn how to bargain in Chinese
To learn about the Chinese currency

生词 New Words

买	mǎi	v	buy
卖	mài	v	sell
送	sòng	v	give sth. as a present; see someone off
找	zhǎo	v	give change; find, look for
能	néng	m.v	can, be able to
行	xíng	adj	all right, OK; competent
便宜	piányi	adj	cheap 便*cheap 宜* yí appropriate
可乐	kělè	n	cola
矿泉水	kuàngquánshuǐ	n	mineral water 矿 mine 泉 spring 水 water
明信片	míngxìnpiàn	n	postcard 信 letter 片 card
光盘	guāngpán	n	CD 光 light, bright
音乐	yīnyuè	n	music 音 sound 乐 music
钱	qián	n	money
小说	xiǎoshuō	n	novel
西方	xīfāng	n	the West
张	zhāng	m.w	for paper, postcards, CDs, etc.
本	běn	m.w	for books
元	yuán	m.w	yuan, basic unit of Chinese currency
角	jiǎo	m.w	jiao, 1/10 of a yuán
分	fēn	m.w	fen, 1/10 of a jiǎo; minute
块	kuài	m.w	a colloquial term for yuán
毛	máo	m.w	a colloquial term for jiǎo
多少	duōshao	q.w	how much; how many
百	bǎi	num	hundred
一共	yígòng	adv	altogether
那	nà	conj	in that case; then

句型 Speech Patterns

Goods	多少钱	Num+MW
可乐 Kělè	多少钱 duōshao qián	一瓶? yì píng?
茶 Chá	多少钱 duōshao qián	一杯? yì bēi?
这/那（个） Zhè/nà(gè)	多少钱 duōshao qián	一个? yí gè?

The pattern on the left is the most popular one to use when asking about the price of something. You may also use: 多少钱 + num + m.w + goods? or, num + m.w + goods + 多少钱?

Goods	How Much	MW
可乐 Kělè	三块钱 sān kuài qián	一瓶。 yì píng.
茶 Chá	两块五 liǎng kuài wǔ	一杯。 yì bēi.
明信片 Míngxìnpiàn	两块五 liǎng kuài wǔ	一张。 yì zhāng.

Answers to price related questions are straightforward. You use the amount of money to replace the question word 多少钱.

Goods	怎么	卖?
可乐 Kělè	怎么 zěnme	卖? mài?
明信片 Míngxìnpiàn	怎么 zěnme	卖? mài?
这（个） Zhè(gè)	怎么 zěnme	卖? mài?

If you are uncertain about what measure word to use for what you wish to buy, you can simply say "goods + 怎么卖?". However, the answer may not be about price, but about the way the goods are sold because the literal meaning of this type of question is "how to sell this?"

S	太	Adj	了
光盘 Guāngpán	太 tài	贵 guì	了。 le.
今天 Jīntiān	太 tài	热 rè	了。 le.
踢足球 Tī zúqiú	太 tài	累 lèi	了。 le.

The construction 太…了 expresses the idea of excessiveness. It is important that 了 is placed after the adjective in this type of construction. The subject here can be a noun or a verbal phrase.

补充词汇 Additional Vocabulary

车票	chēpiào	bus/train ticket	水果	shuǐguǒ	fruits
邮票	yóupiào	stamp	果汁	guǒzhī	fruit juice
电影票	diànyǐngpiào	film ticket	苹果汁	píngguǒzhī	apple juice
地图	dìtú	map	西红柿汁	xīhóngshìzhī	tomato juice
导游图	dǎoyóutú	tourist map	茅台	máotái	Maotai liquor
国画	guóhuà	Chinese painting	青岛啤酒	Qīngdǎo Píjiǔ	Tsingtao beer

对话 1 Dialogue One

买方：请问，可乐多少钱一瓶？

卖方：小瓶的②四块，大瓶的八块。

买方：矿泉水呢？

卖方：两块钱一瓶。

买方：我买一瓶矿泉水。

卖方：好。你还要点儿什么？

买方：有没有明信片？

卖方：有，明信片一块两毛五③一张。你要几张？

买方：我要五张。一共多少钱？

卖方：一共八块两毛五分。

买方：这是十块。

卖方：找你一块七毛五④。谢谢。

对话 2 Dialogue Two

卖方：你好！你想买点儿什么？

买方：这本小说多少钱？

卖方：二十五块。

买方：光盘怎么卖？

卖方：十块钱一张。

买方：有没有中国音乐光盘？

卖方：有。中国音乐、西方音乐，我这儿都有。

买方：十块太贵了，能不能便宜点儿？

卖方：二十张一百块，买一送一，怎么样？

买方：二十张太多了。我买十张，五十块，行不行？

卖方：不行。五十块太少了，六十块吧。

买方：好吧，那就六十块吧。

语法注释 Grammar Notes

① **Chinese currency, 人民币, (￥) is called the "people's currency" or RMB.**
It has three basic currency units:元, 角 and 分.

1元 = 10角   1角 = 10分   1元 = 100分

In Chinese currency, the notes come in denominations of 100元, 50元, 20元, 10元, 5元, 2元, 1元, 5角, 2角,1角, 5分, 2分 and 1分 (but notes in 分 are not issued any more).The coins are the 1元, 5角, 2角, 1角, 5分, 2分 and 1分 coins.

② **小瓶的**— 小瓶的 refers to 小瓶的可乐. Such usage is very common in Chinese.

③ **一块两毛五**— The last unit a price or an amount of money being discussed (分 or 毛) tends to be omitted in spoken Chinese, so the following amounts read separately as

2.50 两块五 (毛)   27.45 二十七块四毛五 (分)

④ **找你一块七毛五**— When giving change, 找 is used. The sentence means "here is your change of 1.75 yuan".

文化知识 Cultural Note

市场上讨价还价 Bargaining in Chinese Markets

Bargaining is common in the markets in China, and it is also possible to bargain in some big shops. A rule of thumb is to look around and see if others are bargaining to see whether it is acceptable where you are shopping. In terms of how much you can counter-offer, you will need to consult locals to get their advice. However, it is very important to remember that you don't bargain for fun. If you are not really interested in the goods, don't start the bargaining process. Of course, it is a different matter if you cannot agree on the price of something with the seller and wish to reach a compromise.

练习 Exercises

口语练习 Speaking Practice

1) **Roleplay. Work in pairs or small groups. Imagine you are in a Chinese market and would like to buy something you see. Take turns acting as the seller and buyer and see if you are able to get a good bargain.**

2) Take turns playing the role of a customer/salesperson/waiter with your group or partner and create a dialogue based on the information given below.

中国书店	
《汉语口语》	22.5元/本
《汉语语法》	49.99元/本
中国地图	18元/张
明信片	1.2 元/张
音乐光盘	20元/张

北京饭店	
烤鸭	168 元/只
红烧肉	42元/盘
炒饭	16元/盘
中国啤酒	15元/瓶
可乐	15元/瓶

听力练习 Listening Practice

Listen to the short dialogues and circle the correct answer in each group, accordingly.

1)	a. 四块	b. 两块五	c. 五块
2)	a. 四张	b. 十张	c. 十四张
3)	a. 八块	b. 五块	c. 五十块
4)	a. 中国音乐	b. 日本音乐	c. 西方音乐
5)	a. 三张	b. 五张	c. 八张
6)	a. 五十一块	b. 五十块	c. 五十五块
7)	a. 十二块	b. 十一块	c. 十块
8)	a. 中国饭馆便宜	b. 中国饭好吃	c. 中国饭馆贵

语法练习 Grammar Practice

1. Multiple choice.

1) 明信片 ＿＿＿＿ 卖?

    a.怎么   b.什么   c.多少

2) 一杯可乐 _____ ?

    a.多少   b.多少钱   c.是多少

3) 一瓶可乐和两瓶矿泉水 _____ 二十八块五。

    a.一起   b.有   c.一共

4) 你们 _____ 学汉语的光盘？

    a.是不是   b.有没有   c.想不想

5) _____ 便宜点儿？

    a.行不行   b.能不能？   c.会不会？

6) 语法书多少钱一 _____ ?

    a.张   b.只   c.本

2. Choose the right question or answer to fill in each blank in the following dialogues. The first one has been done as an example.

    a. 光盘多少钱一张？   b. 能不能便宜点儿？

    c. 一共多少钱？   d. 你想买点儿什么？

    e. 矿泉水怎么卖？   f. 找你两块二。

1) A: <u>光盘多少钱一张？</u>

    B: 九块钱一张。   (a)

2) A: 你好！_____

    B: 请问，你们有没有音乐书？   ( )

3) A: 我要五张明信片，_____

    B: 一共十二块。   ( )

4) A: 五十块太贵了，_____

    B: 四十五怎么样？   ( )

5) A: _____

    B: 小的五块钱一瓶，大的十块。   ( )

6) A: 这是五十块。

    B: 谢谢，_____   ( )

认字识词 Words with Known Characters

Figure out the English meanings of each of the words below and write them in the spaces provided.

口语	_____	语法	_____
写信	_____	写作	_____
名片	_____	图片	_____
泉水	_____	暖水瓶	_____
共和国	_____	买卖	_____
前方	_____	后方	_____

翻译练习 Translation

Say the following sentences in Chinese first, and then write them out in characters.

1) How much is it for a glass of beer?
2) 15 yuan for a CD is too expensive. Could it be made a bit cheaper?
3) I want to buy a CD of Chinese music. I like Chinese music very much.
4) How much is this book?
5) The big bottles are 5 yuan each and small ones 3 yuan each.
6) How much is it altogether for one bottle of beer and two bottles of cola?

阅读 Reading

中国人买汽车

　　在中国，一瓶啤酒只要五块钱左右，一只北京烤鸭也只要七八十块钱。中国吃的、喝的都很便宜，可是有的 (some) 东西 (thing) 很贵，中国的房子 (house) 和汽车就很贵。

　　中国人以前 (before) 钱不多，大家 (all) 都骑自行车。现在 (now) 不少的人都有汽车，因为大家都比以前有钱。有的人钱很多，他们不买中国车，他们买外国车。外国车比中国车贵多了。还有的人非常 (exceptionally) 有钱，他们不喜欢开便宜的外国车，他们喜欢开外国<u>名车</u> (brand name car)。外国名车非常贵。在中国，现在开外国名车的<u>大多</u> (mostly) 是商人和律师，开中国车的大多是医生和老师，骑自行车的大多是工人和学生。

Please answer the following questions based on the information in the above text.

1) What kind of things are cheap in China?

2) Why did most Chinese use bicycles before?

3) What was the major difference between the local Chinese and foreign cars?

4) What kinds of people buy the brand name foreign cars in China?

5) Who are the bicycles users nowadays?

汉字知识 Chinese Characters

偏旁 Radicals

The semantic associations of three radicals are given in the table below. Can you work out and write their related characters according to the pinyin provided?

亻	single person	nǐ	tā	zuò	xìn	lún
氵	water	jiǔ	kě	qì	méi	fǎ
囗	enclosure	tú	huí	guó	yīn	yuán

汉字笔顺 Stroke Order

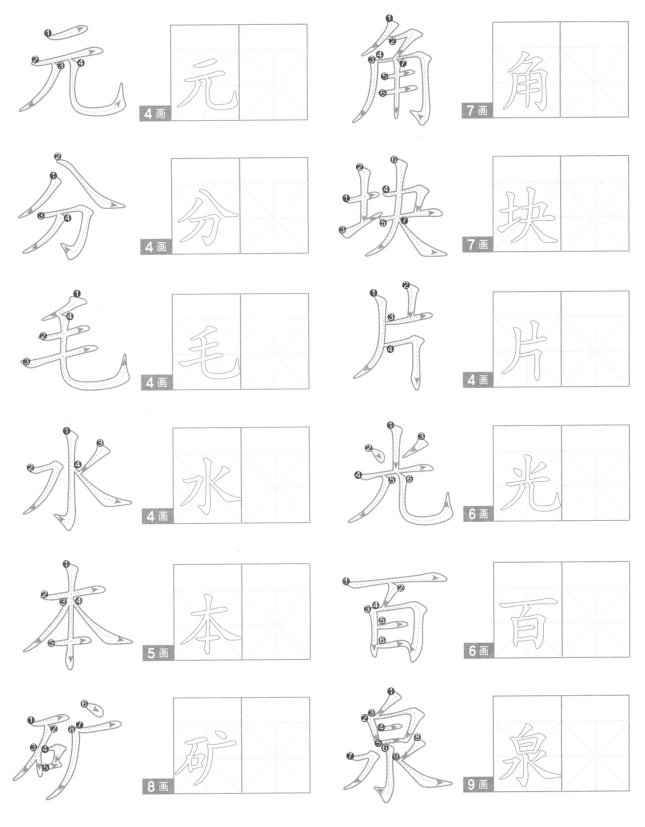

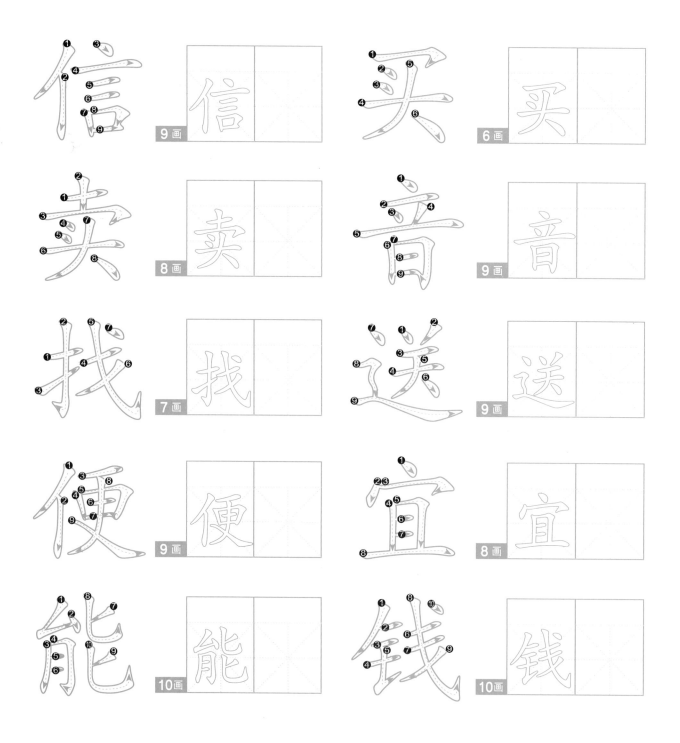

13

第十三课　　餐厅几点开门？

Learning objectives

Learn to tell time
Learn to ask when shops/services open and close
Two ways to ask about the time

生词 New Words

开始	kāishǐ	v	start, begin	始 begin
上课	shàngkè	v-o	have classes	课 lesson
开门	kāimén	v-o	open	门 door
关门	guānmén	v-o	close	关 close; turn off
交换	jiāohuàn	v	exchange	交 cross; make　换 change
差	chà	v	lack, be short of	
点	diǎn	n	o'clock	
早饭	zǎofàn	n	breakfast	
学校	xuéxiào	n	school, college	校 school, college
餐厅	cāntīng	n	canteen	餐 food, meal　厅 hall
时候	shíhou	n	time; when	时 time; hour　候* hòu time
上午	shàngwǔ	n/t.w	morning	午 noon
下午	xiàwǔ	n/t.w	afternoon	
现在	xiànzài	n/t.w	now	现 now
刻	kè	n	quarter (hour)	
半	bàn	n	half	
水果店	shuǐguǒdiàn	n	fruit shop	水果 fruit　果 fruit
苹果	píngguǒ	n	apple	苹* apple
日本	Rìběn	p.n	Japan	
小时	xiǎoshí	n	hour	
附近	fùjìn	n	nearby	附 attach, add　近 close, near
斤	jīn	m.w	Chinese weight unit equal to ½ kilogram	
新	xīn	adj	new	
这么	zhème	adv	so	
差不多	chàbuduō	adj/adv	similar; nearly, almost	
左右	zuǒyòu	adv	about, approximately	

句型 Speech Patterns

（现在）	几点	（了）?
	几点 Jǐ diǎn	了? le?
现在 Xiànzài	几点 jǐ diǎn	了? le?
现在 Xiànzài	几点? jǐ diǎn?	

Please note that the question word 几 (not 什么) is used in questions for which the answers will be numbers (see the next speech pattern). The use of 了 indicates a present-completed state.

（现在）	N 点	N（分）
（现在） (Xiànzài)	十点 shí diǎn	十五（分）。 shí wǔ(fēn).
（现在） (Xiànzài)	七点 qī diǎn	一刻。 yíkè.
（现在） (Xiànzài)	十一点 shí yì diǎn	半。 bàn.

Telling time is easy and straight forward in Chinese. 是 is not necessary except for the sake of emphasis or confirmation of what has been mentioned in an earlier statement.

S	几点	V O?
图书馆 Túshūguǎn	几点 jǐdiǎn	开门? kāimén?
银行 Yínháng	几点 jǐdiǎn	关门? guānmén?
你 Nǐ	几点 jǐdiǎn	吃早饭? chī zǎofàn?

As before, the time element goes before the verb. 几点 is used to ask for a specific time, similar to "what time" in English.

S	什么时候	V O?
你 Nǐ	什么时候 shénme shíhou	去北京? qù Běijīng
书店 Shūdiàn	什么时候 shénme shíhou	开门? kāimén?
水果店 Shuǐguǒ diàn	什么时候 shénme shíhou	关门? guānmén?

什么时候 is a more general enquiry about time, similar to "when" in English.

补充词汇 Additional Vocabulary

起床	qǐchuáng	get up		吃午饭	chī wǔfàn	have lunch
睡觉	shuìjiào	go to bed		吃晚饭	chī wǎnfàn	have supper
休息	xiūxi	have a break		橘子	júzi	orange
下课	xiàkè	end class		香蕉	xiāngjiāo	banana
下班	xiàbān	finish work		梨	lí	pear
洗澡	xǐzǎo	have a shower/bath		葡萄	pútao	grape

◎◎ 对话 1 Dialogue One

张亮：　　请问，现在几点？

李大明：十点三十五分。你是新来的交换学生②吧？

张亮：　　对。我叫张亮。

李大明：我叫李大明。

张亮：　　你们几点开始上课？

李大明：九点。

张亮：　　这么晚！你们几点吃早饭？

李大明：八点左右。

张亮：　　学校里面有没有餐厅③？

李大明：有。餐厅早上不开门。上午差一刻十一点开门④。

张亮：　　几点关门？

李大明：晚上六点。

张亮：　　图书馆几点开门？

李大明：图书馆上午八点半开门，晚上十点半关门。

张亮：　　谢谢。

对话2 Dialogue Two

张亮：你好，我是新来的交换学生。

学校附近有水果店吗?

王京：有，学校东面就有一家。

张亮：水果店什么时候关门?

王京：水果店二十四小时都开，不关门。

张亮：太好了，谢谢。

这儿的苹果贵不贵?

王京：不贵。

苹果一斤四块钱左右⑤。

张亮：有没有英国苹果?

王京：没有。有日本苹果。

张亮：日本苹果多少钱一斤?

王京：日本苹果差不多十块钱一斤。

语法注释 Grammar Notes

① **Reading clock in Chinese**—The Chinese use the words 点 (hour) and 分 (minute) to indicate a certain time when telling time using a clock. As in English, Chinese also has quarter hours (刻) and half hours (半). 差 is used in Chinese to express the notion of "to". Its patterns are 差一刻Y点 or Y点差一刻.

1:00	一点
1:15	一点一刻；一点十五分
1:30	一点半；一点三十分
1:45	一点三刻；一点四十五分；差一刻两点；两点差一刻
2:05	两点(零，líng)五分
2:13	两点十三分

② **新来的交换学生**—的 here is an attributive marker, and together with the preceding element it forms a modifier for the following noun phrase. So the phrase means "the newly arrived exchange student".

③ **学校里面有没有餐厅?** —学校里面 is a location phrase used here as the subject. This is commonly used in Chinese to indicate the existence or appearance (or disappearance) of something in a location/place.

④ **上午差一刻十一点开门**— When telling time, Chinese uses different time words such as 上午 and 晚上 to refer to particular periods of the day. However, when using a 24-hour clock to tell time, these words are unnecessary.

5:16 am	早上五点十六分	(五点十六分)
9:25 am	上午九点二十五分	(九点二十五分)
12:00	中午十二点	(十二点)
4:30 pm	下午四点半	(十六点三十分)
9:55 pm	晚上九点五十五分	(二十一点五十五分)

⑤ **左右, 差不多**—These phrases both mean "about" in English, but 左右 is placed after a time word, while 差不多 is placed before a word, just like "about" in English.

文化知识 Cultural Note

中国的营业时间 Business Hours in China

Shops and department stores are open for much longer hours in China than in the West. Many restaurants and shops are open till midnight or the early hours in the morning; some are even open 24 hours a day. Weekends are the peak periods for shops and restaurants as many people go shopping or eat out at that time. Services such as banks and post offices are open during the daytime, but ATM is available nowadays in urban areas.

练习 Exercises

口语练习 Speaking Practice

1) Working in pairs, tell your partner about some of your daily routines.

时间	Time	Activities
上午		
下午		
晚上		

2) Talk about the opening and closing times of your local shops or library or pub, etc.

听力练习 Listening Practice

1. Listen to the recording and fill in the correct times on the clocks.

图1   图2   图3   图4

2. Listen to the short dialogues and circle the correct answer in each group, accordingly.

1) a. 十点四十   b. 四点十四   c. 四点十分   (   )

2) a. 早上七点一刻 b. 晚上七点半   c. 早上七点半   (   )

3) a. 晚上十点半   b. 晚上十一点半 c. 上午十点半   (   )

4) a. 七块六一斤   b. 一块九一斤   c. 七块九一斤   (   )

5) a. 差一刻十点   b. 八点四十五   c. 九点四十五   (   )

6) a. 十二点   b. 十三点   c. 十五点   (   )

7) a. 八点三十   b. 九点三十   c. 十点三十   (   )

8) a. 十一点半   b. 十二点半   c. 一点半   (   )

语法练习 Grammar Practice

1. Multiple choice.

1) 请问，现在 _____ ？

　　a. 几点   b. 多少点   c. 什么点？

2) 餐厅 _____ 八点开门。

　　a. 中午   b. 下午   c. 早上

3) 图书馆 _____ 开门。

　　a. 星期一上午八点半   b. 八点半上午星期一

　　c. 上午八点半星期一

4) 苹果三块五一 _____ 。

　　a. 张   b. 斤   c. 只

5) 现在十 _____ 半。

　　a. 刻   b. 分   c. 点

6) 我们 _____ 一刻一点吃午饭。

　　a. 差   b. 在   c. 是

2. Put the words in each group in the correct order to create sentences.

1) 六十八块   五   北京烤鸭   一盘

2) 开门   天天   上午   商店   八点半

3) 回家   你   坐车   几点

4) 有   一个   家   我   小   水果店   附近

5) 认识   不   那个   交换学生   汉字

6) 关门   九点   晚上   图书馆   星期六

认字识词 Words with Known Characters

Figure out the English meanings of each of the words below and write them in the spaces provided.

课本	_____	课外	_____
门口	_____	大门	_____
换钱	_____	校车	_____
近期	_____	学期	_____
新年	_____	新生	_____
开关	_____	交朋友	_____

翻译练习 Translation

Say the following sentences in Chinese first, then write them out in characters.

1) What time is it now? It is a quarter to twelve.

2) What time does the British Library open on Sundays?

3) How much is a *jin* of apples?

4) A *jin* of apples is 2 yuan and eighty fen.

5) Our library opens at half past seven in the morning and closes at ten in the evening.

6) He is very busy with work and goes home at eight in the evening almost every day.

阅读 Reading

图书馆开放 (open) 时间 (time)
fàng

东南大学是一个很大的大学，有十个学院。学校有东、西两个校园 (campus)，东校园是老 (old) 校园，西校园是新校园。两个校园都有图书馆。医学、商学、文学、语言学的书都在东校园图书馆，其他 (other) 的书都在西校园的新图书馆。下面是两个图书馆的开放时间。

东南大学图书馆开放时间

星期	东图书馆	西图书馆
星期一——星期四	08:00 – 22:00	08:00 – 22:00
星期五	08:00 – 20:00	08:00 – 20:00
星期六	上午：08:30 – 12:00 下午：13:00 – 17:00	上午：08:30 – 12:00 下午：13:00 – 17:00
星期日	上午：休息(xiūxi) closed 下午：13:00 – 17:00	上午：09:00 – 13:00 下午：休息　closed

Please answer the following questions based on the information in the above text.

1) If one needs to borrow medical books, which library should one go to?

2) Is it possible to borrow books from the East Library at 9:30 at night on a Monday?

3) Can one read in the West Library all day on Saturdays?

4) If one needs to borrow a book from the East Library on Saturday, is that service available during lunchtime?

5) Are there any services available on Sundays at either of the libraries?

汉字知识 Chinese Characters

偏旁 Radicals

The semantic associations of three radicals are given in the table below. Can you work out and write their related characters according to the pinyin provided?

讠	speech	kè	xiè	shuí	qǐng	shuō	yǔ
木(朩,木)	wood	bēi	xiào	lǐ	běn		
艹	grass	cài	píng	chá	yīng		

汉字笔顺 Stroke Order

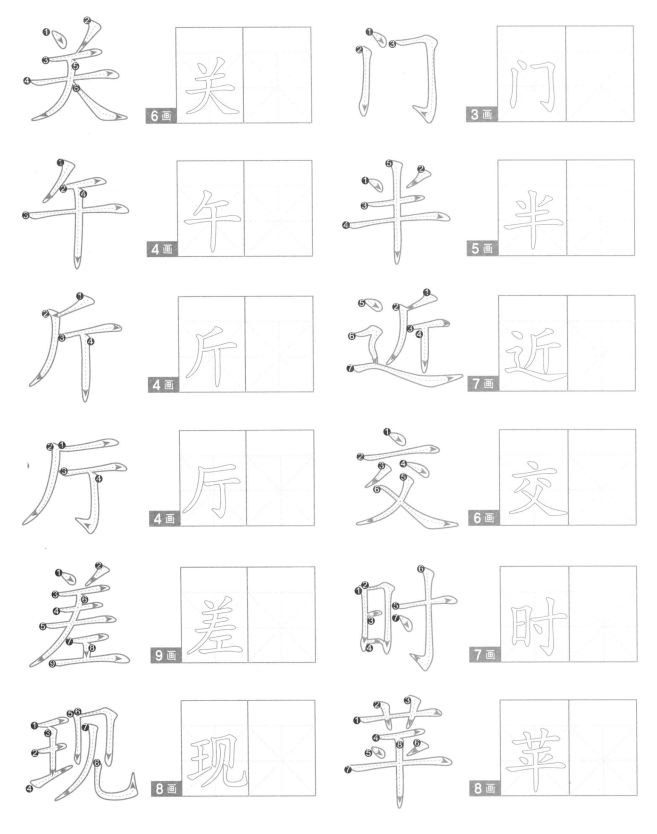

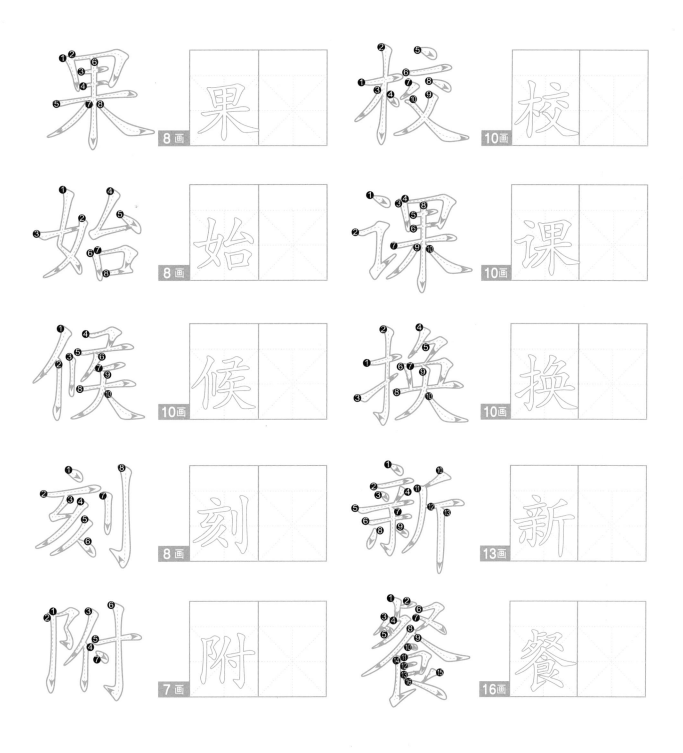

14

第十四课   走路去医院要几分钟？

Learning objectives

To learn to say how long it takes to get to somewhere nearby
To learn to give more detailed directions to places
To learn how to see a doctor

生词 New Words

可以	kěyǐ	m.v	may; can	以 with, according to
要	yào	v/m.v	need, want; should	
拐	guǎi	v	turn	
疼	téng	v	hurt, pain	
感冒	gǎnmào	v/n	catch cold; cold 感 be affected; feel 冒 risk
发烧	fāshāo	v	have a fever 发 become; develop
打针	dǎzhēn	v-o	inject 针 needle
休息	xiūxi	v	rest, break 休 cease 息 xī rest
红绿灯	hónglǜdēng	n	traffic lights 绿 green 灯 light
分钟	fēnzhōng	n	minute 钟 clock
十字路口	shízì lùkǒu	n	crossroad
药店	yàodiàn	n	pharmacy 药 medicine, drug
药方	yàofāng	n	prescription 方 prescription
饭后	fànhòu	n	after a meal
开水	kāishuǐ	n	boiled/boiling water 开 boil
舒服	shūfu	adj	comfortable 舒* easy 服 fú be accustomed to
不舒服	bù shūfu	adj	unwell, uncomfortable
片	piàn	m.w	for tablets
次	cì	m.w	times (for verbs)
然后	ránhòu	conj	then 然 thus, so
一直	yìzhí	adv	straight forward 直 straight
第*	dì	prefix	for ordinal numbers
从	cóng	prep	from
向	xiàng	prep	towards
到	dào	prep/v	to; arrive

句型　Speech Patterns

去	Place	怎么	走?
去 Qù	医院 yīyuàn	怎么 zěnme	走? zǒu?
去 Qù	商店 shāngdiàn	怎么 zěnme	走? zǒu?
去 Qù	学校 xuéxiào	怎么 zěnme	走? zǒu?

怎么走 is used to ask for directions to get somewhere, regardless of whether you walk or drive there.

到	Place	向	LW	拐
到 Dào	十字路口 shízì lùkǒu	向 xiàng	左 zuǒ	拐。 guǎi.
到 Dào	红绿灯 hónglǜdēng	向 xiàng	右 yòu	拐。 guǎi.
到 Dào	十字路口 shízì lùkǒu	向 xiàng	东 dōng	拐。 guǎi.

Please note the word order, which is: you reach a place first, and then face the direction in which you are going before you turn.

从	A	到	B	Manner	要 Time
从 Cóng	我家 wǒ jiā	到 dào	学校 xuéxiào	走路 zǒulù	要十分钟。 yào shí fēnzhōng.
从 Cóng	学校 xuéxiào	到 dào	商店 shāngdiàn	骑车 qíchē	要五分钟。 yào wǔ fēnzhōng.
从 Cóng	学校 xuéxiào	到 dào	车站 chēzhàn	开车 kāichē	要一刻钟。 yào yí kè zhōng.

This sentence pattern could be altered to 从 A + Manner + 到 B 要 + Time, e.g., 从我家走路到学校要十分钟. The alternative pattern places more emphasis on the manner or method of moving from A to B.

S	MV	Adv	V	O
你 Nǐ	要 yào	多 duō	喝 hē	水。 shuǐ.
你 Nǐ	要 yào	好好 hǎohāo	休息。 xiūxi.	
你 Nǐ	应该 yīnggāi	多 duō	说 shuō	汉语。 Hànyǔ.

In Chinese, some adjectives can function as adverbs, such as 多 and 好好. 好好 here means both "more" and "well".

补充词汇　Additional Vocabulary

大门	dàmén	gate, entrance	头晕	tóuyūn	feel dizzy
动物园	dòngwùyuán	zoo	头疼	tóuténg	headache
中医院	zhōngyīyuàn	hospital using TCM	牙疼	yáténg	toothache
机场	jīchǎng	airport	肚子疼	dùziténg	stomach ache
游乐场	yóulèchǎng	theme park	腰疼	yāoténg	backache
停车场	tíngchēchǎng	car park	腿疼	tuǐténg	pain in the leg

🎧 对话 1 Dialogue One

问路人: 请问，去第一医院①怎么走?

路人: 你一直向前走，到红绿灯向右拐。

问路人: 然后呢?

路人: 走到第三个十字路口再向左拐，左边就是第一医院。

问路人: 谢谢。走路要几分钟?

路人: 要二十分钟左右②。

问路人: 有公共汽车吗?

路人: 有。可以坐 325 路③去。

问路人: 坐车要几分钟?

路人: 坐车只要五分钟。

问路人: 一共要坐几站?

路人: 四站。

问路人: 谢谢。

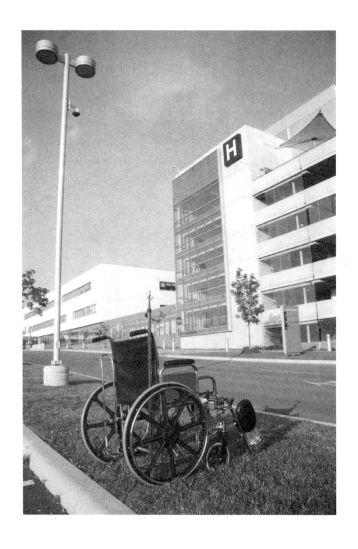

对话 2 Dialogue Two

医生：　王小姐，你哪儿不舒服？

王小英：我头疼。

医生：　发烧吗？

王小英：不发烧。

医生：　我看看。你有点儿感冒。打一针吧。

王小英：医生，我不想打针，吃药可以吗？

医生：　你想吃中药还是吃西药？

王小英：我想吃西药。

医生：　好，这是你的药方。你要④好好休息，多喝开水。

王小英：谢谢。这药怎么吃？

医生：　一日三次，一次两片，饭后吃⑤。

王小英：对不起，附近有药店吗？

医生：　有，对面就有一个。

语法注释 Grammar Notes

① 第一医院——第一 is an ordinal number. Chinese ordinal numbers are formed by adding the prefix 第 to numbers.

For example:	
第一	第一中学
第二	第二餐厅
第三十五	第三十五中学

② （从这儿去第一医院走路）要二十分钟左右——For periods of time, just as in English, the number precedes the unit of measure.

5 minutes	五分钟
1 quarter of an hour/15 minutes	一刻钟/十五分钟
half an hour	半(个)小时/三十分钟

1 hour	一 (个) 小时/一个钟头
2 hours	两 (个) 小时/两个钟头
3 hours and 6 minutes	三 小时零六分
3 hours and 15 minutes	三 小时十五分/ 三个钟头零一刻
3 and a half hours	三个半小时/三个半钟头

③ 325路（公共汽车）—325路 refers to the number/route of a bus service. As in English, in Chinese 325 is read as "three two five" because the number is more than two digits. However, you should read 25 路 as "èr shí wǔ lù" as the number is only two digits long.

④ 要— Like many Chinese characters, 要 has more than one meaning. In addition to "want", it also means "need" as in 走路要几分钟, or "need/should" as in 你要好好休息，多喝开水.

⑤ **Instructions for taking medicine** —饭前 (before a meal), 饭后 (after a meal), and 一日三次 (three times a day) are common phrases one encounters when listening to or reading instructions on how to take medicine.

文化知识 Cultural Note

在中国问路
Asking for Directions in China

If you ask for directions in the northern part of China, especially in rural areas, people will probably give you an answer by using 东, 南, 西 and 北 rather than 左 or 右. This is partly because it is easy to figure out one's position by either looking at the sun or the direction most houses face. While people giving directions in urban areas will give an estimated walking time to your destination, it is more likely that people in rural areas will give you a rough estimate of the distance from where you are to where you are going.

练习 Exercises

口语练习 Speaking Practice

Role play: work in pairs and use the following information to describe "your" experience of visiting a doctor based on information below.

Time	Symptoms	Doctor's Prescription	Doctor's	Advice
今天早上	发烧	吃药，打针	休息两天	多喝水
今天上午	头不舒服	吃中药	休息一天	不喝酒
上星期天	感冒	不吃药，也不打针	多休息	多喝水
上星期二	toothache	西药/一日三次/饭后	不喝酒	多喝茶
上星期五	stomach ache	西药/一日两次/饭前	不吃晚饭	不喝酒

听力练习 Listening Practice

Listen to the short dialogues and circle the correct answer in each group, accordingly.

1) a. 第一中学　　b. 第十一中学　c. 第二十一中学

2) a. 想吃西药　　b. 想吃中药　　c. 想打针

3) a. 四十路　　b. 四十四路　　c. 十四路

4) a. 一个小时　　b. 一刻钟　　c. 半个小时

5) a. 骑车十五分钟　　　　　b. 骑车三十分钟

　　c. 骑车四十五分钟

6) a. 一日三次，一次两片　　　b. 一日两次，一次三片

　　c. 一日两次，一次两片

7)   a. 到十字路口向左拐   b. 到红绿灯向右拐

   c. 到十字路口向右拐

8)   a. 饭前两片   b. 饭后两片

   c. 六小时一次，一次两片

语法练习 Grammar Practice

1. Multiple choice.

1)   从这儿走路去医院要三十 __b__ 左右。

   a. 分   b. 分钟   c. 点钟

2)   医生，这药 __c__ 吃？

   a. 什么   b. 应该   c. 怎么

3)   我们应该 __c__ 汉语。

   a. 很说   b. 说多   c. 多说

4)   一直走，到红绿灯 __a__ 右拐。

   a. 向   b. 在   c. 去

5)   你有点儿发烧，打一针 __b__ 。

   a. 吗   b. 吧   c. 呢

6)   医生，我不发烧，我 __c__ 喝啤酒吗？

   a. 应该   b. 想   c. 可以

2. Fill in the blanks with the words given. The first one has been done as an example.

   a. 从   b. 向   c. 在   d. 差不多   e. 左右   f. 可以

1)   从这儿坐车到商店要十分钟。   (a)

2)   到十字路口 __b__ 左拐。   (   )

3)   他喜欢 __c__ 酒馆喝啤酒.   (   )

4)   图书馆九点 __e__ 开门。   (   )

5)   现在 __d__ 三点了。   (   )

6)   你 __f__ 坐地铁去，附近有地铁站。   (   )

认字识词 Words with Known Characters

Figure out the English meanings of each of the words below and write them in the spaces provided.

红茶	_____	绿茶	_____
药水	_____	药片	_____
药酒	_____	开发	_____
休学	_____	休想	_____
公路	_____	铁路	_____
路灯	_____	问路	_____

翻译练习 Translation

Say the following sentences in Chinese first, then write them out in characters.

1) You have got a bit of a cold. You need to have more rest and more water.

2) It is only a 5 minutes' walk from my home to the school.

3) Excuse me, how do I get to the train station?

4) You go straight ahead, and then turn right at the traffic lights.

5) Would you like to take Chinese medicine or Western medicine?

6) How long does it take to walk from the hospital to the chemist?

写作练习 Writing

Write a passage of around 150 characters about your study or work in terms of your daily routine, for instance when you start to study/work each day, for how long you do this and so on.

阅读 Reading

"中国人民很行"

我爸爸在北京工作，去年我去北京看他。有一天，我有点儿感冒，想去药店买点儿药。可是我爸爸那天很忙，不能和我一起去。因为我会

说一点儿汉语，认识几个汉字，所以 (therefore) 我说我一个人去，我能
找到药店。

　　我爸爸说我们家附近就有一个小药店。他说我在第一个十字路口向
右拐，然后到第二个十字路口向左拐，走五分钟，左边就是中国人民银
行，小药店就在银行的旁边。他还说：“要是 (if) 你不认识路，问问中
国人，他们都很喜欢帮助 (help) 人。”

　　我想只要 (so long as) 找到 (find) 中国人民银行，就可以找到药店。可是
我找了 (look for) 半个小时，只看见 (see) 一个“中国人民很行”。我
只好 (have to) 问一个小朋友去银行怎么走。小朋友说：“这不就是银行的
大门吗？”原来 (it turns out)，“中国人民很行”就是“中国人民银行”。

Please answer the following questions based on the information in the above text.

1) Why was his father unable to go with him?

2) Why was he confident that he could find the chemist himself?

3) Where was the chemist located?

4) Why couldn't he find the bank?

5) What does 中国人民很行 mean?

汉字知识 Chinese Characters

偏旁 Radicals

The semantic associations of three radicals are given in the table below. Can you
work out and write their related characters according to the pinyin provided?

火 (灬)	fire	kǎo	dēng	shāo	chǎo	
人 (亻)	person	cóng	jīn	huì	yǐ	gè
心 (忄)	heart / mind	nín	gǎn	xiǎng	zěn	xī

📖 汉字笔顺 Stroke Order

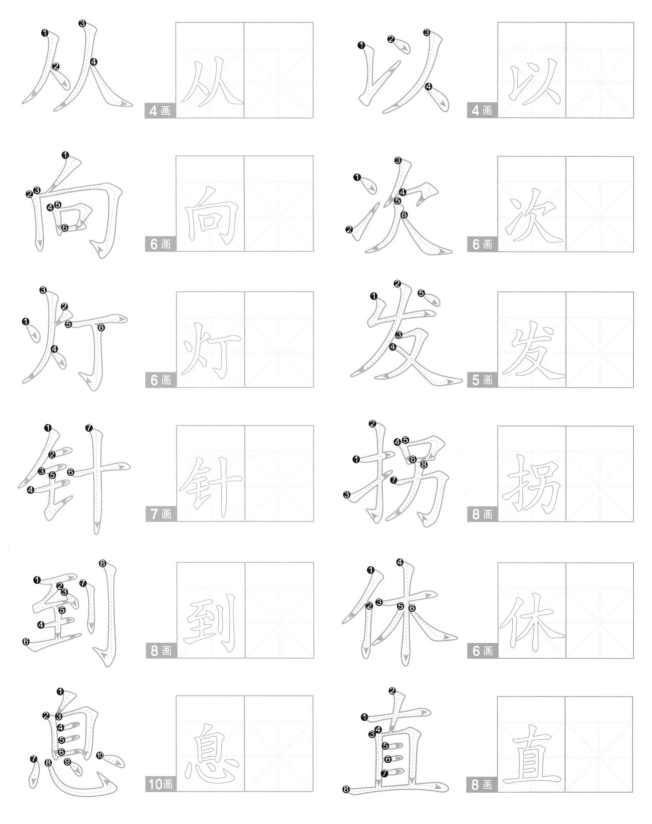

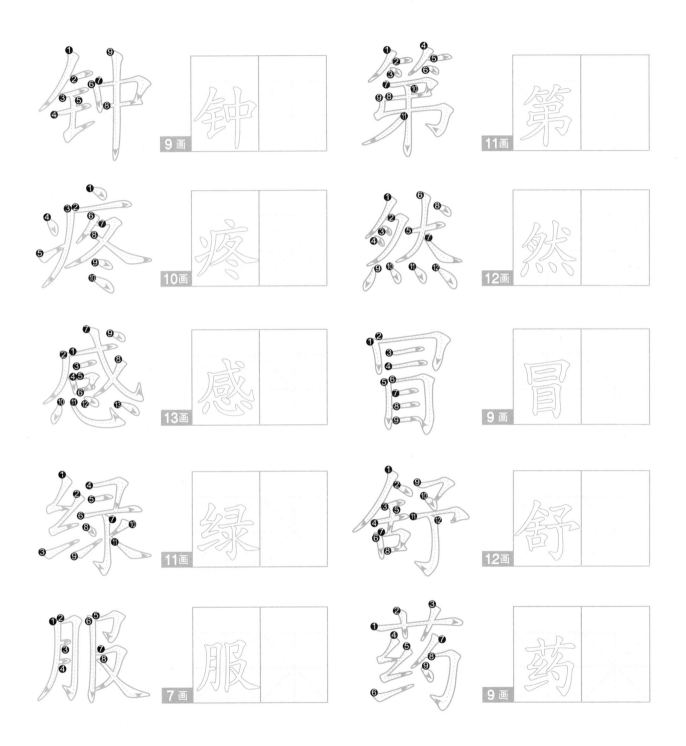

15

第十五课　　英镑上涨了！

Learning objectives

To learn to express a change in terms of state or condition
To learn to contrast the states of affairs in the past and present
To learn to ask about exchange rates and how to exchange currencies

生词 New Words

看病	kànbìng	v-o	see a doctor	病 disease
收	shōu	v	accept; receive	
上涨	shàngzhǎng	v	rise	涨 rise
下跌	xiàdiē	v	fall	跌 fall down
得	děi	m.v	have to	
太极拳	tàijíquán	n	tai chi	极 pole　拳 fist
公斤	gōngjīn	m.w	kilogram	公 prefix for metric units
人民	rénmín	n	people	民 folk, people
人民币	rénmínbì	n	RMB (Chinese currency)	币 currency
欧元	ōuyuán	n	euro	欧 Europe (abbr.)
美元	měiyuán	n	US dollar	美 USA (abbr.); beautiful
英镑	yīngbàng	n	pound sterling	镑 pound sterling
旅行	lǚxíng	n	travel	旅 travel
支票	zhīpiào	n	cheque	支 pay　票 ticket
现金	xiànjīn	n	cash	金 gold
以前	yǐqián	n	before, ago	
昨天	zuótiān	n	yesterday	昨* last, in 昨天 and 昨晚
已经	yǐjīng	adv	already	已 already　经 through
很少	hěn shǎo	adv	seldom	
那么	nàme	adv	so	
既…也…	jì … yě …	conj	… as well as …	
零	líng	num	zero	
千	qiān	num	thousand	

句型 Speech Patterns

S	Adv	Adj/V/VO	了
天气 Tiānqì		冷 lěng	了。 le.
英镑 Yīngbàng	已经 yǐjīng	上涨 shàngzhǎng	了。 le.
她 Tā	不 bù	打太极拳 dǎ tàijíquán	了。 le.

了 at the end of a sentence after either an adjective or a verb can indicate a change of state or condition as compared to a previous situation. Note that the negative form in the last sentence 不...了 means "not any more".

S	Adv	V	O	了
我 Wǒ	已经 yǐjīng	吃 chī	药 yào	了。 le.
他 Tā	昨天 zuótiān	去 qù	北京 Běijīng	了。 le.
我们 Wǒmen		买 mǎi	中文书 zhōngwén shū	了。 le.

了 at the end of a sentence with an action verb usually implies that an action has been accomplished and that there has been a change of condition or status as a result of that action.

S	Adv	没(有)	V	O
英镑 Yīngbàng		没 méi	上涨。 shàngzhǎng.	
他 Tā		没 méi	去 qù	北京。 Běijīng.
小王 Xiǎo Wáng	昨天 zuótiān	没 méi	打 dǎ	太极拳。 tàijíquán.

If an action is not completed or realised, 没有 is used to negate the verb and 了 is not required. Note its difference with 不...了.

Num	A Currency	换	Num	B Currency
100	美元 měiyuán	换 huàn	630	元人民币。 yuán rénmínbì.
100	欧元 ōuyuán	换 huàn	847	元人民币。 yuán rénmínbì.
100	英镑 yīngbàng	换 huàn	999	块。 kuài.

Since 元 is the unit of many currencies, 人民币 here is used to specify the currency being exchanged. You can put 人民币 after 换 and before the amount of currency B.

补充词汇 Additional Vocabulary

汇率	huìlǜ	exchange rate
外汇	wàihuì	foreign currency
兑换处	duìhuànchù	exchange bureau
日元	rìyuán	Japanese yen
港币	gǎngbì	HK dollar
卢布	lúbù	rouble

瑞士法朗	Ruìshì fǎláng	Swiss franc
克朗	kèlǎng	krone; krona
比索	bǐsuǒ	peso
运动	yùndòng	exercise (physical)
抽烟	chōuyān	smoke
打牌	dǎpái	play cards/mahjong

对话 1 Dialogue One

李东：小王，上星期五^①你怎么没来上课？

王京：我去看病了。我感冒了。

李东：你吃药了吗？

王京：吃了。

李东：现在天气冷了，
感冒的人^②也多了。

王京：去医院看病的人^②也多了。

李东：你得多休息两天^③。

王京：我现在已经好了。小李，你比以前瘦了？

李东：我是瘦了一点儿^④。我以前太胖了。

王京：你现在多少公斤？

李东：六十五公斤，比以前瘦了五公斤。

王京：我现在很少去打网球，你还天天去打吗？

李东：我现在不^⑤打网球了，我打太极拳了。

对话 2 Dialogue Two

王小英：请问，一百美元换多少人民币？

李先生：六百三十块。

王小英：不是能换六百三十七块吗^⑥？

李先生：昨天能换那么多，
今天美元下跌了。

王小英：一百英镑能换多少人民币？

李先生：九百九十九块。英镑上涨了，欧元也上涨了。

王小英：一百欧元能换多少块?

李先生：八百四十七块。

王小英：我换五百欧元。你们收不收旅行支票?

李先生：收，我们既收旅行支票，也收现金⑦。

语法注释 Grammar Notes

① 上星期五——上 is used to indicate a previous perod of fime (or "last"), while 下 refers to a future fime (or "next"). The following table provides more details on relevant time words.

Before the last	Last	This	Next	After the next
前天	昨天	今天	明天	后天
前年	去年	今年	明年	后年
大上个月	上(个)月	这(个)月	下(个)月	大下个月
大上个星期	上(个)星期	这(个)星期	下(个)星期	大下个星期
←————————————Past	Now	Future————————————→		

② 感冒的人 and 看病的人—— These two phrases mean "people who have colds" and "people who see doctors". Attributive clauses will be discussed in Lesson 19. At the moment, you may take them as "people with colds" and "people seeing doctors".

③ 你得多休息两天——得 and 应该 have similar meanings, however 得 differs from 应该 in that it implies that one has to act as if there isn't any alternative.

For example:
医生说你应该多吃菜，少吃肉。
我太累了，我得休息一会儿。

Also, 得 is never used in the negaive, i.e., you cannot say 不得. Also, 两天 means "a couple of days", not necessarily just two days.

④ 我是瘦了一点儿—是 is used here as a confirmation of a comment made by the other speaker who said, "你比以前瘦了".

⑤ 不 and 没—不 is used for negation of both present and future actions, while 没 is usually used to negate past actions, indicating that the action did not take place or has not been completed. Please note the differences between the last two sentences.

    1) 他明天不去北京。   He is not going to Beijing tomorrow.
    2) 他昨天没去北京。   He didn't go to Beijing yesterday.
    3) 他不去北京了。   He is not going to Beijing as planned.

⑥ 不是能换六百三十七块吗?—This is a rhetorical question used for confirmation. The speaker believes that the amount should be 637 rather than 630.

⑦ 我们既收支票，也收现金 — The expression 既 ... 也 ... refers to two separate actions in the sense of both ... and, or ... as well as ....

> **For example:**
> 他既会说英语，也会说法语。

文化知识 Cultural Note

"胖""瘦"的含义转变
The Changing Connotations of 胖 and 瘦

While it is still common to hear Chinese people say 你胖了 or 你瘦了 to each other, the two sentences are understood very differently nowadays. 你胖了 used to be considered a compliment, as it was often a sign of someone having an affluent and comfortable life. On the other hand, 你瘦了 used to be imply that someone had a physical problem (as the character has an "illness" radical). Nowadays however, many would be only too pleased to hear that they appear to be slimmer. This is an example of how the connotations of words can change over a period of time in the Chinese language.

练习 Exercises

口语练习 Speaking Practice

1. Role play. Imagine that you are going to China for a holiday. The following table lists some of foreign currency exchange rates (unit: 100). Choose a currency from one country or region and try to change a reasonable amount of money into RMB for your trip.

英国	英镑	100	10.00	84.78	63.05
中国	人民币	999.59	100	847.33	630.10
法国	欧元	117.917	11.80	100	74.36
美国	美元	156.68	15.86	134.47	100

2. Work in pairs. Tell your partner:

1) Three things that you used to do, but do not do any longer (using 不 ... 了).

2) Five things that did not take place, such as you didn't go to work yesterday (using 没).

听力练习 Listening Practice

Listen to the short dialogues and circle the correct answer in each group, accordingly.

1) a. 打针   b. 吃药   c. 既吃药也打针

2) a. 五公斤   b. 六公斤   c. 七公斤

3) a. 打太极拳   b. 打网球   c. 打篮球

4) a. 六块   b. 六块一   c. 六块五

5) a. 欧元   b. 英镑   c. 美元

6) a. 没吃晚饭   b. 没吃午饭   c. 没吃早饭

7) a. 六千七百元   b. 五千七百元   c. 五千一百元

8) a. 现在瘦   b. 以前瘦   c. 现在和以前一样

语法练习 Grammar Practice

1. Multiple choice.

1) 昨天很热，今天天气 _____ 了。

   a. 冷　　　　　b. 热　　　　　c. 好

2) 去年我七十公斤，现在八十公斤了。我 _____ 了。

   a. 瘦　　　　　b. 很胖　　　　c. 胖

3) 100美元 _____ 820元人民币。

   a. 是　　　　　b. 有　　　　　c. 换

4) 我们既爱吃中国菜，_____ 。

   a. 也喝中国酒　b. 也爱喝中国酒　c. 和喝中国酒

5) 换钱应该去 _____ 。

   a. 大使馆　　　b. 银行　　　　c. 商场

6) 英镑 _____ 下跌，美元下跌了。

   a. 没有　　　　b. 不　　　　　c. 是

2. Fill in the blanks with the words given.

   a. 以前　b. 没有　c. 得　d. 应该　e. 不　f. 可是

1) 张先生 _____ 会说汉语，可是现在不会说了。　（　）

2) 医生说我发烧了，明天 _____ 在家休息。　（　）

3) 我有旅行支票，_____ 他们只收现金。　（　）

4) 你是病人，不 _____ 喝酒。　（　）

5) 他病了，_____ 吃早饭。　（　）

6) 我昨天没有打太极拳，我现在 _____ 打太极拳了。（　）

认字识词 Words with Known Characters

Figure out the English meanings of each of the words below and write them in the spaces provided.

生病 _____　　　病人 _____

南极	_____	北极	_____
民间	_____	国民	_____
金币	_____	机票	_____
门票	_____	车票	_____
经常	_____	非常	_____

翻译练习 Translation

Say the following sentences in Chinese first, then write them out in characters.

1. It is December now. The weather has turned cold.

2. I used to play football, but now I do tai chi instead.

3. How many US dollars can be exchanged for 100 pounds sterling?

4. The Chinese food in London is both inexpensive and delicious.

5. He is thinner than before.

6. I do not have cash, I only have traveller's cheques.

阅读 Reading

王先生什么时候能去中国？

　　王先生一直 (all the time) 想去中国看看，可是他没有很多钱，所以前几年，他差不多天天都去银行看汇率，希望 (hope) 英镑上涨。可是汇率天天都不一样，今天英镑上涨了，明天人民币上涨了，后天英镑下跌了，大后天美元下跌了。所以王先生一直没有去中国。

　　昨天，我在酒吧里看见他了。他对 (to) 我说他现在不去中国了。我问他为什么不去了，他说现在人民币上涨了，去中国太贵了，他要去美国，因为美元下跌了。我说人民币还要上涨，现在就应该去中国。王先生说："我等 (wait) 下跌了再去。"我对他说："你不要等了，因为你可能要等很长 (long) 时间。"

Please answer the following questions based on the information in the above text.

1) What has Mr Wang been planning to do all this time?

2) What is the hold-up for him?

3) When and where did the narrator meet Mr Wang yesterday?

4) What did Mr Wang tell the narrator and why did he tell him that?

5) What did the narrator say to Mr Wang and why did he say that?

汉字知识 Chinese Characters

偏旁 Radicals					
The semantic associations of three radicals are given in the table below. Can you work out and write their related characters according to the pinyin provided?					

扌	hand				
		huàn	zhǎo	dǎ	guǎi
钅	metal				
		yín	zhēn	qián	zhōng	tiě
彳	step				
		xíng	hén	děi	lù

汉字笔顺 Stroke Order

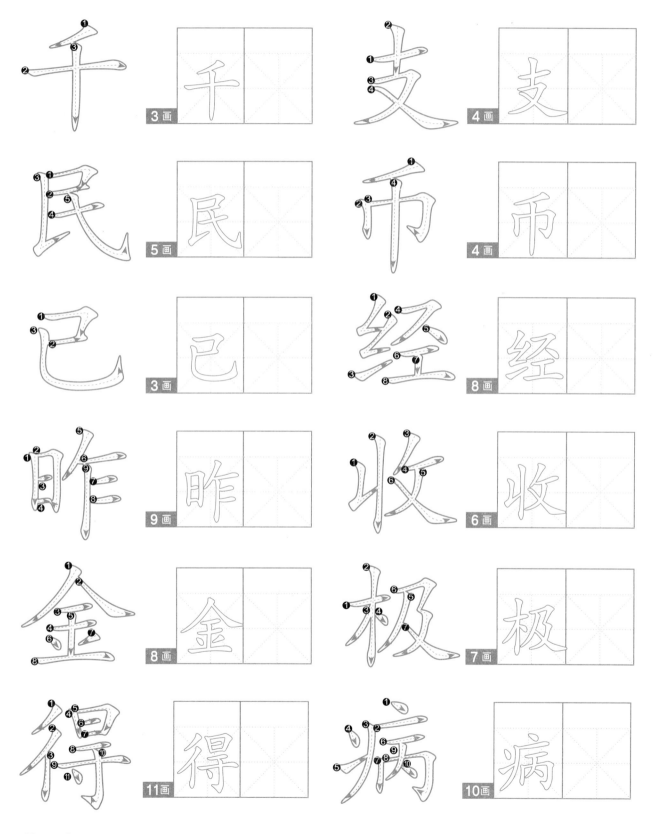

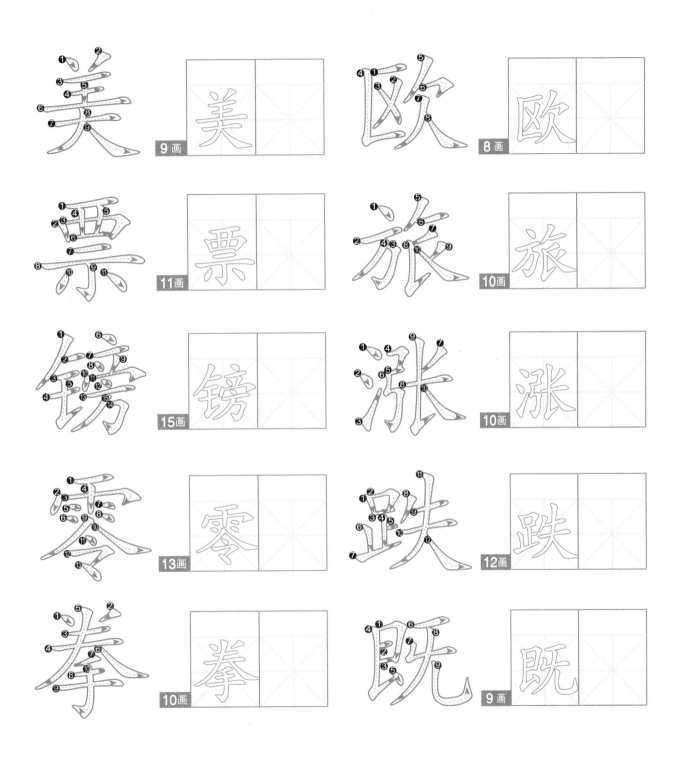

16

第十六课   我是坐公共汽车来的

Learning objectives

To learn to both ask for and give specific information about past actions
To learn to express the length of an accomplished action
To learn to both ask and say how far one place is from another

生词 New Words

让	ràng	v	make, let; ask; allow
等	děng	v	wait
花	huā	v/n	spend, take (time, money); flower
爱	ài	v	love; like very much
需要	xūyào	v	need 需 need
看来	kànlái	v	seem
离开	líkāi	v	depart, leave 离 leave; seperate
出租车	chūzūchē	n	taxi 出租 rent 出 go out 租 rent
比赛	bǐsài	n/v	match; have a match 赛 match, competition
上半场	shàngbànchǎng	n	the first half (of a match) 场 m.w for a match; field
一半	yíbàn	n	half
时间	shíjiān	n	time
坏	huài	adj	out of order; bad; rotten
远	yuǎn	adj	far
久	jiǔ	adj/adv	long time
一定	yídìng	adv	surely, definitely 定 definitely
刚	gāng	adv	just (time)
通常	tōngcháng	adv	usually 通 common, general
有时候	yǒu shíhou	adv	sometimes
总是	zǒngshì	adv	always 总 general, chief
以后	yǐhòu	adv	after, later on, afterwards
真的	zhēn de	adv	really 真 really; true
多长	duō cháng	q.w	how long 长 long
不过	búguò	conj	however 过 pass through, spend
所以	suǒyǐ	conj	so, therefore 所 actually; that which
没关系	méi guānxi	i.e	it doesn't matter 关系 relation 系 tie; department

句型 Speech Patterns

S	Adv	是	Emphasis	V	的
你 Nǐ		是 shì	怎么 zěnme	来 lái	的? de?
我 Wǒ		是 shì	坐出租车 zuò chūzūchē	来 lái	的。 de.
他 Tā	不 bú	是 shì	昨天 zuótiān	去 qù	的。 de.

This pattern is used to emphasise specific information that has been asked for; usually how, when or where a past action took place. While 是 can be omitted in some affirmative statements or questions, but 的 is never left out.

S	是 Emphasis	V	的	O
她 Tā	是打的 shì dǎdí	去 qù	的 de	医院。 yīyuàn.
我 Wǒ	是在英国 shì zài Yīngguó	学 xué	的 de	中文。 Zhōngwén.
我 Wǒ	是昨天 shì zuótiān	见 jiàn	的 de	他。 tā.

If a verb has an object, 的 usually comes before the object, especially in spoken Chinese, though it can also be used at the end of the sentence.

S	V 了	Comp/O
你 Nǐ	学了 xuéle	多长时间? duō cháng shíjiān?
我 Wǒ	学了 xuéle	三个月。 sān gè yuè.
她 Tā	花了 huāle	八镑钱。 bá bàng qián.

When 了 is put immediately after a verb, it emphasises the completion of the action verb.

A	离	B	远/近
你家 Nǐ jiā	离 lí	学校 xuéxiào	远吗? yuǎn ma?
那儿 Nàr	离 lí	车站 chēzhàn	远不远? yuǎn bu yuǎn?
我家 Wǒ jiā	离 lí	商店 shāngdiàn	很近。 hěn jìn.

This construction is used to ask or express how close or far A is from B. Please note the word order is different from that in English.

补充词汇 Additional Vocabulary

球迷	qiúmí	ball game fan		球员	qiúyuán	ball game player
球票	qiúpiào	ball game ticket		裁判	cáipàn	referee
球场	qiúchǎng	ball game court		比	bǐ	to (referring to the game scores)
足球场	zúqiúchǎng	football pitch		赢	yíng	win
网球场	wǎngqiúchǎng	tennis court		输	shū	lose
球队	qiúduì	team		平	píng	draw (in a game)

对话 1 Dialogue One

王京：　　对不起，我来晚了。让你久等了①。

李小英：没关系。我也是刚到。

王京：　　今天地铁坏了，你是怎么来的？

李小英：我是坐公共汽车来的。

王京：　　你坐了多长时间？

李小英：我坐了一个多小时②。你是怎么来的？

王京：　　我是坐出租车来的。

李小英：坐出租车一定很贵。你家离学校远不远？

王京：　　我家离学校很近，我只花了八镑钱。

李小英：你通常怎么来学校？

王京：　　我很少坐出租车。有时候骑车，有时候走路。

对话 2 Dialogue Two

王京：小李，你昨天去没去看足球比赛③？

李东：去了。不过我只看了上半场。

王京：你不是很爱看足球比赛吗？

李东：昨天我是和我女朋友一起去的，
　　　她看了一半就不想看了。

王京：我以前也总是和我女朋友一起去看④&⑤。

李东：现在呢？

王京：我现在没有女朋友了。

李东：真的？是不是因为你太爱看足球，所以她离开你了？

王京：对。她说我不需要女朋友，足球就是我的女朋友。

李东：看来以后我也不能常去看足球赛了⑥。

语法注释 Grammar Notes

① **让你久等了**—让 means "make" here. It also means "allow" or "ask" in colloquial Chinese.

> **For example:**
> a. 我爸爸不让我买汽车。
> b. 老师让我们明天早点儿来。

② **我坐了一个多小时**— This sentence means "it took me over an hour". The pattern is "number + m.w + 多 (+ n)". If the number is around 20, 30, or 50 etc. the pattern is "number + 多 + m.w (+ n)".

> **For example:**
> 三块多（钱）　　八岁多　　两杯多
> 三十多块（钱）　八十多岁　二十多杯

③ **你昨天去没去看足球比赛？**— When using colloquial expressions, you can put 没有 at the end of sentence to form a yes-no question:

> **For example:**
> 你昨天去看足球赛了没有？
> Normally you would have to add 了 before 没有.

④ **总是**— The following words are given in the order of frequency starting from "always"（总是）and ending with "never"（从不）.

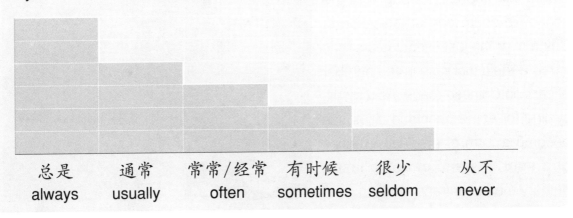

总是	通常	常常/经常	有时候	很少	从不
always	usually	often	sometimes	seldom	never

⑤ 我以前也总是和我女朋友一起去看——以前 here means "in the past", therefore the verb following it describes the past, like "used to" in English. It implies that a condition has changed.

For example:

a. 我以前常去酒吧喝酒。　（我现在不常去了。）
b. 以前我不喜欢吃牛肉。　（现在我喜欢吃了。）

⑥ 看来以后我也不能常去看足球赛了——以后 here means "in the future", therefore the verb following it describes the future. It implies that the present condition is different from what is going to happen.

For example:

a. 我以后要去中国工作。(我现在不在中国工作。)
b. 以后我不喝可乐了。(我现在喝可乐。)
看来 here functions like "it seems" in English but in Chinese "it" is not needed here. Similarly, there is no "it" in 是不是.
因为你太爱看足球，所以她离开你了？

文化知识 Cultural Note

中国的自行车　Bicycles in China

China used to be referred to as the kingdom of bicycles. The number of bicycles in China reached 500 million in late 1980s, with one bicycle for every two people in China's population. For years, bicycles in China were a part of people's everyday lives and were an important means of transportation. However, while they are still highly visible everywhere, the development of roads and the automobile industry, along with the economic boom and urbanisation of China over the last twenty years, has led to a rapid increase in the number of cars on Chinese roads. As a result, cycling for some people in cities has become a form of physical exercise or a sport instead of being just a primary means of transportation.

练习 Exercises

口语练习 Speaking Practice

1. Working in pairs, ask each other the following questions and make sure that all the questions and answers are understood fully.

1) 你家离学校远不远?

2) 你通常怎么来学校?

3) 今天你是怎么来学校的?

4) 你是几点到学校的?

5) 你在大学是学什么专业的?

6) 今天你想几点回家?

2. Working in small groups, use frequency words (always, often, usually, never etc.) to talk about activities you do and activities that you used to do.

听力练习 Listening Practice

Listen to the short dialogues and circle the correct answer in each group, accordingly. Each dialogue has two questions.

1)	a. 骑自行车	b. 坐公共汽车	c. 走路
2)	a. 一个小时	b. 一个多小时	c. 两个小时
3)	a. 二十多分钟	b. 三十分钟	c. 半个多小时
4)	a. 坐地铁	b. 坐公共汽车	c. 骑自行车
5)	a. 踢足球	b. 看足球赛	c. 去酒吧
6)	a. 电视坏了	b. 女朋友来了	c. 不喜欢看
7)	a. 他不爱她	b. 他爱狗	c. 狗和女朋友他都爱
8)	a. 有新男朋友了	b. 他爱猫	c. 他很爱狗

语法练习 Grammar Practice

1. Multiple choice.

1) 上个月我是和朋友一起去北京 _____ 。

    a. 了　　　　b. 的　　　　c. 的了

2) 那个英国人很爱吃烤鸭，去饭馆 _____ 要点北京烤鸭。

    a. 一定　　　b. 一起　　　c. 是

3) 他的工作总是很忙，很少晚上十点 _____ 回家。

    a. 刚　　　　b. 以前　　　c. 以后

4) 对不起，我来晚了，_____ 地铁坏了。

    a. 可是　　　b. 看来　　　c. 因为

5) 我昨天 _____ 在家吃的晚饭。

    a. 不是　　　b. 没　　　　c. 不

6) 我家 _____ 学校很远。

    a. 离　　　　b. 和　　　　c. 比

2. Complete the following dialogues with the words provided.

1) Q: 今天早上你是怎么来学校的？

    A: _____。(坐地铁)

2) Q: 你是在哪儿学的中文？

    A: _____。(伦敦大学)

3) Q: 你是什么时候开始学中文的？

    A: _____。(去年九月)

4) Q: 你学了多久了？

    A: _____。(一年半了)

5) Q: 你上个星期是和谁一起去学校学中文的？

    A: _____。(我女朋友)

6) Q: 你和你女朋友是在哪儿认识的？

    A: _____。(在大英图书馆)

认字识词 Words with Known Characters

Figure out the English meanings of each of the words below and write them in the spaces provided.

爱国	_____	爱人	_____
交通	_____	远东	_____
等车	_____	赛车	_____
近视	_____	远视	_____
出生	_____	出口	_____
商场	_____	总共	_____

翻译练习 Translation

Say the following sentences in Chinese first, then write them out in characters.

1) How did you come here this morning? We came by bus.

2) He used to take taxis a lot, but now he seldom does so.

3) The school is not far from the shop. It only takes 10 minutes on foot.

4) It seems that they arrived last night.

5) It was in China that we met.

6) I don't often go to football matches now as my wife doesn't like to watch them.

阅读 Reading

我们是在法国认识的

去年的新年我是在法国过 (pass) 的。我去法国看我奶奶 (grandmother)。我是坐飞机去的。下了飞机以后，我去找行李 (luggage) 车，一位非常漂亮的女孩 (girl) 也在找。我没有和她说话。

第二天，我和我奶奶去商店买东西 (shopping)，我又 (again) 看见了那个女孩。她也看见了我。我问她是哪国人，她说她是英国人。我又问她是什么地方人，她说她是伦敦人。我说我也是伦敦人，我在北伦敦

工学院 (polytechnic) 上学。
她说她也是北伦敦工学院
的学生，她家离学院很
近，就在学院旁边。我们
两个都是英国人，都在一
个学校里上学，可是她不
认识我，我也不认识她。
我们是在法国认识的。现
在她是我的女朋友。

Please answer the following questions based on the information in the above text.

1) Where did the writer spend last New Year and why?

2) How did he get there and what happened upon his arrival?

3) Who did he see when he went out shopping with his grandmother the following day?

4) What did he learn about the girl?

5) What has happened since then?

汉字知识 Chinese Characters

偏旁 Radicals

The semantic associations of three radicals are given in the table below. Can you work out and write their related characters according to the pinyin provided?

辶 walk	zhè	biān	yuǎn	jìn	tōng
土 (圡, 坴) soil	dì	huài	chǎng	kuài	zuò
王 (玉) king; jade	qiú	bān	xiàn		

📖 汉字笔顺 Stroke Order

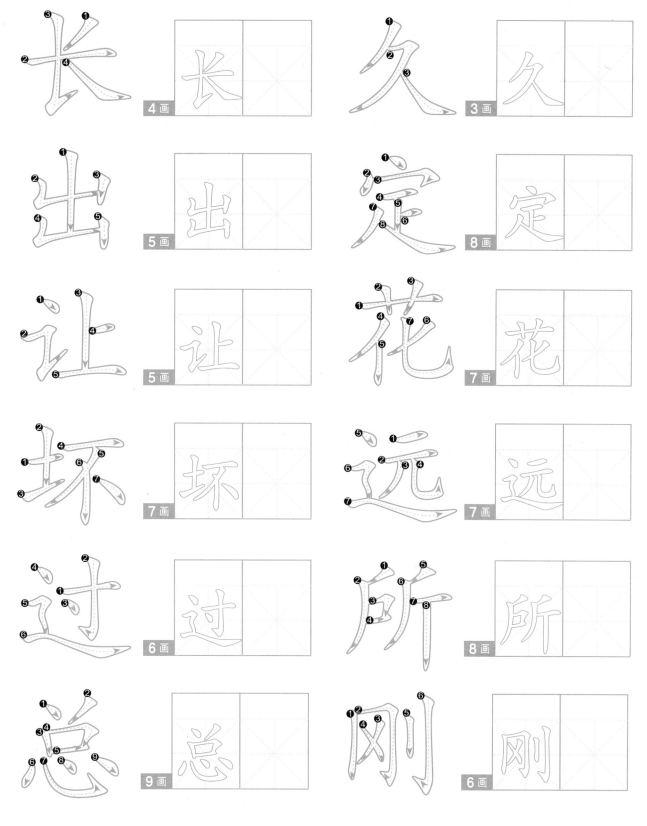

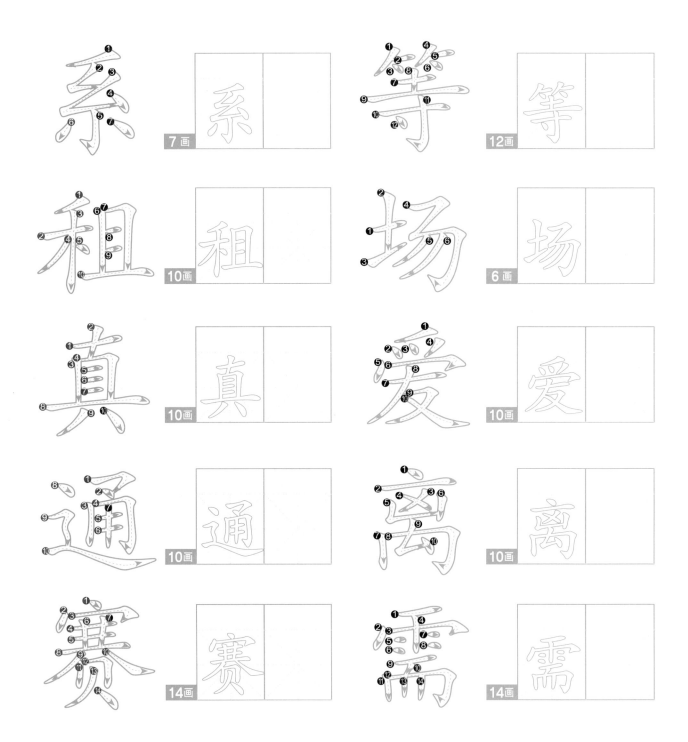

系 7画
等 12画
租 10画
场 6画
真 10画
爱 10画
通 10画
离 10画
赛 14画
需 14画

17

第十七课　　你普通话说得很流利

Learning objectives

Learn to comment on an action using the verb complement 得
Learn the uses of verb complements of state and manner
Learn the use of duration expressions in V-O constructions

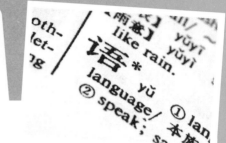

生词 New Words

跳舞	tiàowǔ	v-o/n	dance	跳 jump	舞 dance
表演	biǎoyǎn	v/n	perform; performance	表 show	演 perform
成功	chénggōng	v/n	succeed; success	成 succeed; become	功 achievement
唱歌	chànggē	v-o	sing	唱 sing	歌 song
容易	róngyì	adj	easy		
开晚会	kāi wǎnhuì	v-o	have an evening party	开会 attend/hold a meeting	
信	xìn	v	believe		
流利	liúlì	adj	fluent	流 flow	利 sharp; benefit
不错	búcuò	adj	correct; not bad, pretty good	错 wrong, incorrect	
普通	pǔtōng	adj	ordinary, common	普 ordinary	
普通话	pǔtōnghuà	n	Mandarin, common speech	话 speech	
功夫	gōngfu	n	kong fu (Chinese martial art)	夫 fū man; husband	
懂	dǒng	v	understand		
怪不得	guàibude	adv	no wonder	怪 blame; strange	
才	cái	adv	not ... until, only		
极	jí	adv	extremely		
从来不	cóngláibù	adv	never	从来 always, all along	
得	de	pt	verb complement marker		
跟	gēn	prep/v/conj	with; from; follow; and		
啊	a	pt	ah (exclamation of surprise, etc.)		
回头见	huítóu jiàn	i.e	see you later		
遍	biàn	m.w	times (for verbs)		
还	hái	adv	even; in addition		
不怎么样	bù zěnmeyàng	i.e	not up to much		

句型 Speech Patterns

S	V	得	Comp
你 Nǐ	说 shuō	得 de	很好。 hěn hǎo.
他 Tā	跳 tiào	得 de	不错。 búcuò.
晚会 Wǎnhuì	开 kāi	得 de	怎么样? zěnmeyàng?

The 得 complement follows right after a verb and comments on the performance or result of that verb. The complement can be further modified by an intensifier such as an adverb of degree 很.

S	(V)	O	V	得	Comp
你 Nǐ	(说) (shuō)	普通话 pǔtōnghuà	说 shuō	得 de	很好。 hěn hǎo.
他 Tā	(跳) (tiào)	舞 wǔ	跳 tiào	得 de	很好。 hěn hǎo.
他 Tā	(写) (xiě)	汉字 Hànzì	写 xiě	得 de	好不好? hǎo bu hǎo?

The first verb in this speech pattern can be omitted, as shown on the left.

S	V 了	Duration	(的)	O
你 Nǐ	学了 xuéle	一年 yì nián	(的) (de)	中文。 Zhōngwén.
我 Wǒ	喝了 hēle	一晚上 yì wǎnshang	(的) (de)	酒。 jiǔ.
他 Tā	看了 kànle	两个小时 liǎng gè xiǎoshí	(的) (de)	书。 shū.

In a V-O construction, if the verb refers to a durative action, the duration expression can be inserted between the verb and its object to form an attributive for the object.

S	TW	才/就	V(O)	了
他 Tā	五点 wǔ diǎn	就 jiù	来 lái	了。 le.
妈妈 Māma	早上 zǎoshang	就 jiù	走 zǒu	了。 le.
他 Tā	五点 wǔ diǎn	才 cái	来。 lái	

才 and 就 can be used to indicate different views about the time when a certain action took place. 就 stresses the immediateness of the verb action while 才 means "not until". 了 is not used with 才 in this pattern.

补充词汇 Additional Vocabulary

节目	jiémù	programme (show)	迪斯科	dísikē	disco
话剧	huàjù	play	弹钢琴	tán gāngqín	play the piano
歌剧	gējù	opera	弹吉他	tán jíta	play the guitar
京剧	jīngjù	Peking opera	拉小提琴	lā xiǎotíqín	play the violin
音乐剧	yīnyuèjù	musical play	有意思	yǒu yìsi	interesting
芭蕾舞	bāléiwǔ	ballet	没意思	méi yìsi	boring

对话 1 Dialogue One

王京：你好，可以请你跳舞吗？

李红：啊，你会说普通话！

王京：我说得不太流利。

李红：你说得很不错。你学了多长时间的中文？

王京：我学了半年了。

李红：学了半年就说得这么好，真不容易！你是在哪儿学的？

王京：对不起，你说得太快了，我不懂，请你再说一遍^①。

李红：我说你的中文说得很好，你是在哪儿学的？

王京：我是在伦敦大学学的。

李红：你学了几本中文书了？

王京：我才学了一本。不过我女朋友是上海人。

李红：怪不得^②你中文说得这么^③好！

对话 2 Dialogue Two

王京：　　小李，昨天晚上的晚会开得怎么样？

李小英：开得很成功。

　　　　大明还唱了一个中国歌儿。

王京：　　真的？他唱得好不好？

李小英：他唱得好极了^④。

　　　　方英舞跳得也很好。

王京：　　你跳舞跳得也不错，

　　　　你跳了没有？

李小英：没有。我跳得不怎么样。

我表演了中国功夫。

王京：　我从来不知道你会中国功夫。

你是什么时候开始学的?

李小英：我半年以前就开始学了⑤。

王京：　你是跟谁学的⑥?

李小英：我是跟张亮学的。

王京：　张亮? 他那么瘦还会中国功夫?

李小英：你不信? 他一个人能打十个人。

王京：　真的? 我早就想⑦学中国功夫了,

我现在就去找他。回头见⑧。

语法注释 Grammar Notes

① **请你再说一遍**— This means, "please say it once again." 一遍 means "once", and 再 means "again" or "once more". This is a way to express repetition.

> For example:
> 我想再看一遍。

② **怪不得** — This is very close to "no wonder" in English, both in meaning and in its position in the sentence, hence 你是法国人, 怪不得你法语说得这么好.

③ **这么** — This is similar to 那么. It expresses pretty much the same idea as "so", but 那么 also suggests a sense of distance from the speaker (cf. 他是法国人, 怪不得他法语说得那么好).

④ **他唱得好极了** — 极了 means "extremely" and it should be put after the adjectives it modifies.

> For example:
> 烤鸭好吃极了。

⑤ **我半年以前就开始学了**—以前 here modifies 半年 and must come after the time expression. If the time expression is a length of time, 以前 means "ago", if the time expression is a point in time, 以前 means "before".

> **For example:**
>
> 我半年以前就开始学了。 (I started to learn it half a year ago.)
> 她六点以前就来了。 (She came before six o'clock.)

⑥ **你是跟谁学的?** —跟 is different from 和 in that it has more than one meaning. It could mean "with" as well as "from" (in the sense of "following"). Thus 跟 and 和 are interchangeable in the first example below, but not in the second example.

> **For example:**
>
> a. 我明天跟我女朋友一起去中国。
> ＝我明天和我女朋友一起去中国。
> b. 我跟李老师学中文。
> ≠我和李老师学中文。

⑦ **早就想** — This means that one would have liked to have done something a long time ago, but for some reason hasn't been able to do so and now may finally be able to do it.

> **For example:**
>
> 我早就想学中文了。
> (I have been meaning to learn Chinese for a long time.)

⑧ **回头见** — This is an alternative colloquial expression for 一会儿见 or 再见.

文化知识 Cultural Note

中国人对赞美的反应 Chinese Reaction to Compliments

Chinese people's reactions to compliments may sometimes surprise Western people as Chinese seem to refute all compliments they receive, an action that is often referred to as Chinese modesty. If you say 你英语说得很好 to a Chinese person who speaks very good English, please do not be surprised if you receive the reply of 我说得一点儿都不好 or the more interesting expression 哪里, 哪里. This is a Chinese way of acknowledging your compliment. Chinese modesty requires replies to compliments to imply that there is still much room for improvement.

练习 Exercises

口语练习 Speaking Practice

1. Working in pairs, ask your partner questions according to the example and the vocabulary provided.

A: 你会说法语吗?　　　B: 会，我会说法语。

A: 你法语说得怎么样? B: 我说得不很好。

会	跳舞	好
喜欢	说中文	流利
爱	看电视	多
喜欢	骑车	快
爱	打网球	好

2. Tell each other something you can do and how well you can do it.

听力练习 Listening Practice

Listen to the short dialogues, and circle the correct answer in each group, accordingly. Each dialogue has two or three questions.

1) a. 生日晚会　b. 中国新年晚会　c. 中文晚会　　　（　　　）

2) a. 星期天晚上 b. 前天晚上　　　c. 昨天晚上　　（　　　）

3) a. 中国功夫　b. 唱歌　　　　　c. 跳舞　　　　（　　　）

4) a. 唱歌　　　b. 跳舞　　　　　c. 唱中国歌　　（　　　）

5) a. 唱中文歌　b. 打太极拳　　　c. 表演功夫　　（　　　）

6) a. 书店　　　b. 图书馆　　　　c. 商学院　　　（　　　）

7)　a. 很好　　　　b. 不好　　　　c. 不怎么样　　　（　　　　）

8)　a. 法学院　　　b. 伦敦大学　　c. 商学院　　　　（　　　　）

语法练习　Grammar Practice

1. Multiple choice.

1)　你怎么 _____ 来，晚会已经开始了。

　　a. 才　　　　　b. 就　　　　　c. 只

2)　他家离学校很近，坐公共汽车一刻钟 _____ 到了。

　　a. 才　　　　　b. 就　　　　　c. 只

3)　我们的中文老师英语、法语都说 _____ 很流利。

　　a. 的　　　　　b. 得　　　　　c. 是

4)　她太极拳打得很好，她是 _____ 一位中国老师学的。

　　a. 跟　　　　　b. 在　　　　　c. 去

5)　王京唱歌 _____ 得不错。

　　a. 很　　　　　b. 唱　　　　　c. 唱歌

6)　对不起，你说得太快了，请你再说 _____。

　　a. 一会儿　　　b. 一边　　　　c. 一遍

2. Use the words provided in brackets to re-write the following sentences.

1)　图书馆星期六十点半才开门。　　　　　　　　（就）

2)　我们下个星期才开始上课。　　　　　　　　　（就）

3)　足球赛五点半就开始了。　　　　　　　　　　（才）

4)　我今天早上七点就吃早饭了。　　　　　　　　（才）

5)　他舞跳得极好。　　　　　　　　　　　　　　（极了）

6)　王先生汉语说得极流利。　　　　　　　　　　（非常）

认字识词 Words with Known Characters

Figure out the English meanings of each of the words below and write them in the spaces provided.

流行 _____ 歌星 _____

说话 _____ 电话 _____

海边 _____ 海菜 _____

公海 _____ 大海 _____

跳高 _____ 跳远 _____

舞厅 _____ 舞会 _____

翻译练习 Translation

Say the following sentences in Chinese first, then write them out in characters.

1) You speak Chinese really well, much better than I do.

2) How is his driving? It is not bad.

3) How long have you studied Chinese? I have studied for a year and half.

4) They came as early as 6:30 this morning. No wonder they are very tired.

5) How could you come so late? They arrived half an hour ago.

6) We all know that learning Chinese is not easy.

阅读 Reading

李大明普通话说得真好

李大明是英国伦敦人，可是他普通话说得很好。一个英国人普通话怎么说得这么好？他是怎么学的呢？

原来，前年夏天李大明和朋友一起去中国玩^{wán}儿 (be on holiday)。那时候他的汉语不怎么样。在一个饭馆里，他说要吃鱼^{yú} (fish)，可是服务员^{fú wù yuán}

(waiter) 给了他一盘鸡 (chicken)。他们应该十号离开饭店，可是饭店要他们四号就离开。他很生气，可是这都是因为他发音 (pronounce) 发得不好。

回到英国以后，他开始认真 (seriously) 学习中文，现在去中国饭馆点菜再也不会错了。大明现在有女朋友了，她是香港 Xiānggǎng (Hong Kong) 人，可是她的普通话还没有大明说得好。

Please answer the following questions based on the information in the above text.

1) Where is Daming from?

2) When did he go to China?

3) What were the problems he encountered during his trip to China?

4) What was the cause of those problems?

5) Where is his girlfriend from?

汉字知识 Chinese Characters

偏旁 Radicals

The semantic associations of three radicals are given in the table below. Can you work out and write their related characters according to the pinyin provided?

白（白）	white	bǎi	quán	de	
足（⻊）	foot	tī	diē	tiào	gēn
禾（禾）	crop	qiū	hé	zū	lì

汉字笔顺 Stroke Order

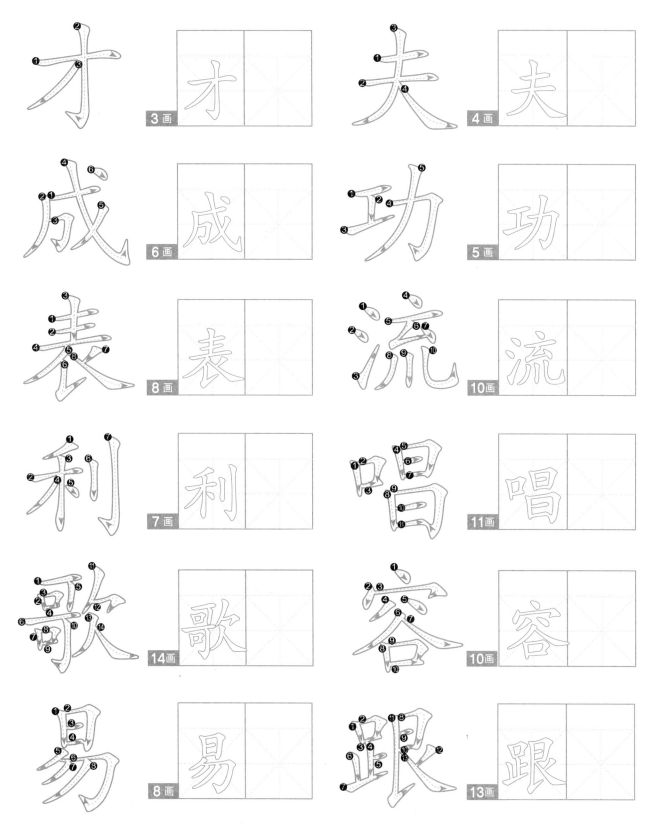

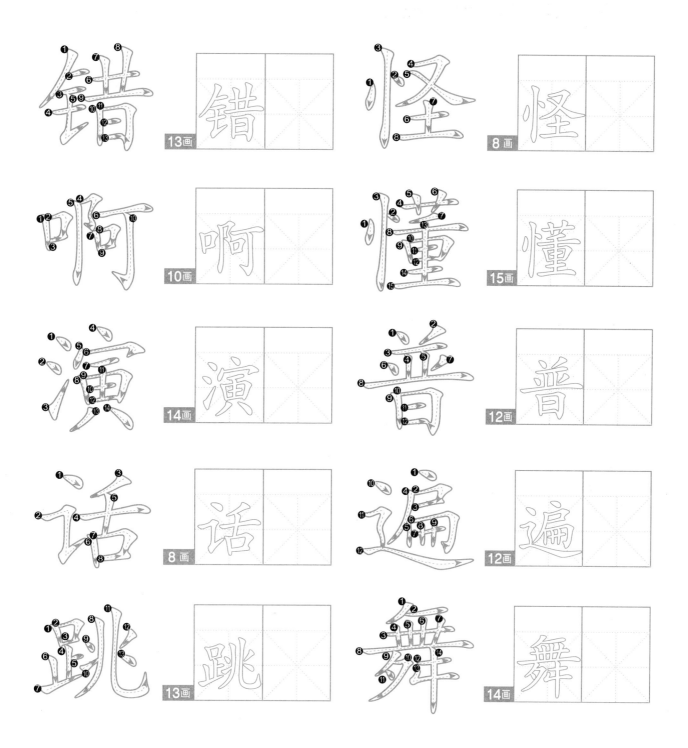

错 13画
怪 8画
啊 10画
懂 15画
演 14画
普 12画
话 8画
遍 12画
跳 13画
舞 14画

18

第十八课   你在干什么呢？

Learning objectives

To learn to talk about currently continuous activities
To learn to talk about continuous activities in the past
To learn to talk about two concurrent activities

生词 New Words

干	gàn	v	do (colloquial)
给	gěi	v	give
打电话	dǎ diànhuà	v	make a telephone call
打工	dǎgōng	v	work as a casual worker
以为	yǐwéi	v	assume (wrongly); think
睡觉	shuìjiào	v/n	sleep
接	jiē	v	meet; connect
用	yòng	v/prep	use; with
帮	bāng	v	help
准备	zhǔnbèi	v/n	prepare; preparation
借	jiè	v	borrow; lend
考试	kǎoshì	v	take an exam
事	shì	n	matter; business
练习	liànxí	n/v	exercise
饭馆儿	fànguǎnr	n	restaurant
口试	kǒushì	n	oral exam
笔试	bǐshì	n	written exam
情书	qíngshū	n	love letter
字典	zìdiǎn	n	dictionary
问题	wèntí	n	question, problem
电子	diànzǐ	n	electronics
最近	zuìjìn	adv	recently
正	zhèng	adv	just then, at that point
一下	yíxià	adv	for a while, briefly; once
一边儿…一边儿…	yìbiānr…yìbiānr…	conj	while … while … (linking two concurrent activities)
对了	duìle	i.e	oh, yes

电话 telephone

睡 sleep   觉 nap, sleep

准 adjust 备 prepare

考 test, inspect 试 test; try

练 practise   习 practise

笔 pen, pencil

情 affection, feeling

典 decree; classics

题 topic; title

子* noun suffix

最 most

句型 Speech Patterns

S	Adv	在	V	O	(呢)
我 Wǒ	不 bú	在 zài	看 kàn	书。 shū.	
我 Wǒ	正 zhèng	在 zài	看 kàn	书。 shū.	
我 Wǒ	（正在） （zhèngzài）		看 kàn	书 shū	呢。 ne.

在 is a continuation aspect marker and precedes a verb to indicate that an action is in progress. This can be further emphasised by adding 正 before 在. 呢 at the end of a sentence expresses the continuation aspect with a rhetorical tone.

S	一边	V1,	一边	V2
他 Tā	一边 yìbiān	吃饭， chīfàn,	一边 yìbiān	看电视。 kàn diànshì.
她 Tā	一边 yìbiān	走， zǒu,	一边 yìbiān	唱。 chàng.
她 Tā	一边 yìbiān	上学， shàngxué,	一边 yìbiān	工作。 gōngzuò.

The construction 一边 … 一边 is useful to express two concurrent actions.

(S1)	V1 O1	的时候,	(S2)	V2 O2
她 ,Tā	来 lái	的时候， de shíhou,		我正在打电话。 wǒ zhèngzài dǎ diànhuà.
我 Wǒ	上大学 shàng dàxué	的时候， de shíhou,		很喜欢跳舞。 hěn xǐhuan tiàowǔ.
	吃饭 Chīfàn	的时候 de shíhou		不要说话。 bú yào shuōhuà.

… 的时候 means "when" and the whole phrase serves as a time clause.

S	用	Sth	Do	Sth
他 Tā	用 yòng	中文 Zhōngwén	写 xiě	信。 xìn.
我 Wǒ	用 yòng	人民币 rénmínbì	买 mǎi	东西。 dōngxi.
他 Tā	用 yòng	碗 wǎn	喝 hē	酒。 jiǔ.

用 is a preposition here introducing a manner or method in which an action is carried out, thus making it simliar to "with" in English. Note that it always precedes the relevant verb.

补充词汇 Additional Vocabulary

画画儿	huàhuàr	paint		洗碗	xǐ wǎn	wash bowls/dishes
听音乐	tíng yīnyuè	listen to music		洗头	xǐ tóu	wash one's hair
打扫房间	dǎsǎo fángjiān	clean rooms		照相	zhàoxiàng	take photos
玩游戏	wán yóuxì	play games		聊天儿	liáotiānr	chat
写论文	xiě lùnwén	write an essay		吵架	chǎojià	quarrel
找工作	zhǎo gōngzuò	look for a job		化妆	huàzhuāng	make up

对话 1 Dialogue One

李东：小王，你在干什么呢？

王京：我在做练习。

李东：昨天晚上九点左右你在干什么①？

王京：我在②上网。

李东：我给你打电话，可是没人接。
　　　我还以为你睡觉了③。

王京：你找我有事吗④？

李东：我正在用中文写信，
　　　你能不能帮帮我？

王京：你给谁写信？

李东：我的一个中国朋友。

王京：是女朋友吧？你让我帮你写情书，对不对？

李东：不，不是情书，我们才刚刚认识。

王京：好吧，我帮你写。你们是怎么认识的？

李东：我去中国饭馆儿吃饭，她在那儿打工。

王京：她也是学生吗？

李东：对，她一边儿上学，一边儿打工。

对话 2 Dialogue Two

张亮：我们正说你呢，你就来了。

李东：你们在说我什么？

张亮：我们在说不知道你最近在忙什么。

李东：我正在准备考试。

谢红：你什么时候考？

李东：下星期就考。星期一考口试，星期二考笔试。

　　　对了，小张，我正想借你的汉英字典用一下⑤。

张亮：没问题。你什么时候用？

李东：下星期二，考笔试的时候用。

谢红：你的电子字典不能用吗？

李东：张老师说考试的时候不能用。

谢红：几点了？我一点钟要去见张老师⑥。

张亮：现在已经一点了。快去吧，她一定正在等你呢。

语法注释 Grammar Notes

① **昨天晚上九点左右你在干什么？** —The continuation aspect can be associated with any time in the past, present or future.

> **For example:**
> a. 今天上午十点我在给我妈妈打电话。
> b. 我现在正在上网。
> c. 明年这个时候，我在北京学习汉语。

For the negative form of the continuation aspect, 不 is used for future actions, but either 不 or 没 can be used for present or past actions.

> **Compare:**
> a. 今天上午十点我不/没在给我妈妈打电话。
> b. 我现在没/不在上网。
> c. 明年这个时候, 我不在北京学习汉语。

② If there is a location phrase with 在 in a sentence, there is no need for another 在 before the verb.

> **For example:**
> a. 昨天下午三点我在中国银行换钱。
> b. 我现在在家上网。

③ 我还以为你睡觉了 — This means "I thought you had already gone to bed."
还 is here used for the sake of emphasis. 以
为 is used here to indicate that the speaker's
assumption is wrong.

> **For example:**
> **a.** 我以为你去中国了。
> **b.** 他们以为我也是中国人。

④ 你找我有事吗? — Literally this means "what do you want me for?" It is
normally used between friends and colleagues.

⑤ 想借你的汉英字典用一下 — 一下 indicates the briefness of the action. The
same effect can be achieved by repeating the verb:

     a.我看一下你的书，好吗?   = 我看看你的书，好吗?
     b.请你给我们表演一下。   = 请你给我们表演表演。

⑥ 我一点钟要去见张老师 — 要 means "be going to".

> **For example:**
> 他明天要去北京。

文化知识 Cultural Note

中国人看爱情 The Chinese View on Love and Marriage

When Chinese men and women start a relationship,
most of them treat it seriously beause they view it
as a natural progression to marriage. Love at first
sight does exist in China, but many couple reckon
love is an affection for each other and for the
people close to them that develops over the years.
Thus, many factors other than "love at first sight"
are considered when a relationship starts, to ensure that the two parties suit each other
and will enter a successful long-term marriage. Chinese people are also more reserved
in openly showing their affection to their loved ones. Although, this of course is changing
along with the rapid societal changes in China. The divorce rate is also rising in today's
China. However, people still long for true affection, which originates from the traditional
Chinese view of love, epitomised in the legend "The Cowherd and the Weaver Girl".

练习 Exercises

口语练习 Speaking Practice

1) Working in pairs, talk about what you were doing or did at a previous time, such as reading a Chinese book, writing Chinese characters, watching TV, and of course studying Chinese!

2) Working in pairs, take turns to ask one another what they were doing at a particular point in time in the past. See the example below.

Q: 星期天晚上七点你在做什么呢？

A: 我在看电视。

Day	Time	Activities
星期天	晚上七点	（在家）看电视
		（在家）上网
		（在银行）换钱
		（在图书馆）看书
		（在一个中国饭馆）吃午饭
		（跟朋友一起）唱中文歌
		（在学校）做作业

听力练习 Listening Practice

Listen to the short dialogues, and circle the correct answer in each group accordingly. Each dialogue has two or three questions.

1) a. 今年   b. 新年   c. 明年   (   )

2) a. 不认识汉字   b. 认识的汉字少

     c. 不喜欢看明信片   (   )

3) a. 在准备考试   b. 在工作   c. 在做作业   (   )

4) a. 上个星期四   b. 这个星期四   c. 下个星期四   (   )

5)   a. 他语法不行   b. 他汉字不行   c. 他口语不行   （   ）

6)   a. 她在上课   b. 她在睡觉   c. 她在上班   （   ）

7)   a. 一天   b. 两天   c. 三天   （   ）

8)   a. 没准备   b. 准备得很好   c. 准备得不好   （   ）

语法练习 Grammar Practice

1. Multiple choice.

1)   前天晚上十点你在做什么 _____ ？

    a. 了   b. 的   c. 呢

2)   晚上，我喜欢 _____ 吃饭，一边看电视 。

    a. 一边   b. 正   c. 有时

3)   你的日文说得这么好，我还 _____ 你是日本人！

    a. 想   b. 怪不得   c. 以为

4)   我上中学 _____ ，他正在上小学。

    a. 以前   b. 的时候   c. 以后

5)   昨天我女朋友来的时候，我 _____ 打电话。

    a. 正在   b. 一边   c. 正再

6)   老师，这个题能 _____ 英语做吗？

    a. 写   b. 和   c. 用

2. Change the following sentences into their negative forms.

1)   他普通话说得很好。

2)   他看了两遍了。

3)   昨天晚上九点我在看电视。

4)   星期天我写了两个小时的汉字。

5)   今天早上我是坐公共汽车来的。

6)   张先生现在正在开会。

认字识词 Words with Known Characters

Figure out the English meanings of each of the words below and write them in the spaces provided.

爱情	_____	情人	_____
考题	_____	电灯	_____
用功	_____	试用	_____
接见	_____	接近	_____
零钱	_____	借钱	_____
女子	_____	睡美人	_____

翻译练习 Translation

Say the following sentences in Chinese first, then write them out in characters.

1) What are you doing now? I am looking for my book.

2) When I went to see him yesterday, he was making a telephone call to his doctor.

3) It is raining outside. I thought you were not coming today.

4) Recently, I have been preparing for the exam. I have to buy a new dictionary this afternoon.

5) My mother likes to sing while cooking.

6) I wasn't in the meeting yesterday morning at ten, I was having Chinese classes.

写作练习 Writing

Write a story of about 150 characters, giving a detailed account of where, when, how, what and why something happened.

阅读 Reading

小李 "做客" (be a guest)

　　小李和他女朋友小方已经认识半年多了。有一天，小方对他说："我爸爸妈妈想见见你，你星期六中午来我家吃饭吧。"

小李听了非常高兴(happy)。星期六上午他先去商场买了两个礼物(gift)，不到十二点他就坐出租车去小方家了。星期六路上车很多，通常到小方家只需要十分钟，可是那天花了半个多小时。到小方家的时候已经十二点半了。小方对小李说："你怎么才来？我们都在等你呢。"小李以为他们在等他吃饭，可是小方的妈妈说："我们都不饿，你慢慢(slowly)做吧。"小方的爸爸说："我这里有啤酒。你可以一边做饭，一边喝啤酒。"原来小方说他饭做得非常好吃，大家正在等他来做饭呢。

Please answer the following questions based on the information in the above text.

1) What did Xiao Fang say to her boyfriend Xiao Li one day?

2) What did Xiao Li do first on the day before he went for his appointment?

3) When and how did Xiao Li arrive at his girlfriend's house?

4) What did Xao Li's girlfriend and her parents expect him to do?

5) What had his girlfriend said to her parents about Xiao Li?

汉字知识 Chinese Characters

偏旁 Radicals

The semantic associations of three radicals are given in the table below. Can you work out and write their related characters according to the pinyin provided?

忄	heart	máng	kuài	guài	qíng
月 (⺼)	moon; flesh	péng	pàng	qī	fú
疒	illness	bìng	shòu	téng	

汉字笔顺 Stroke Order

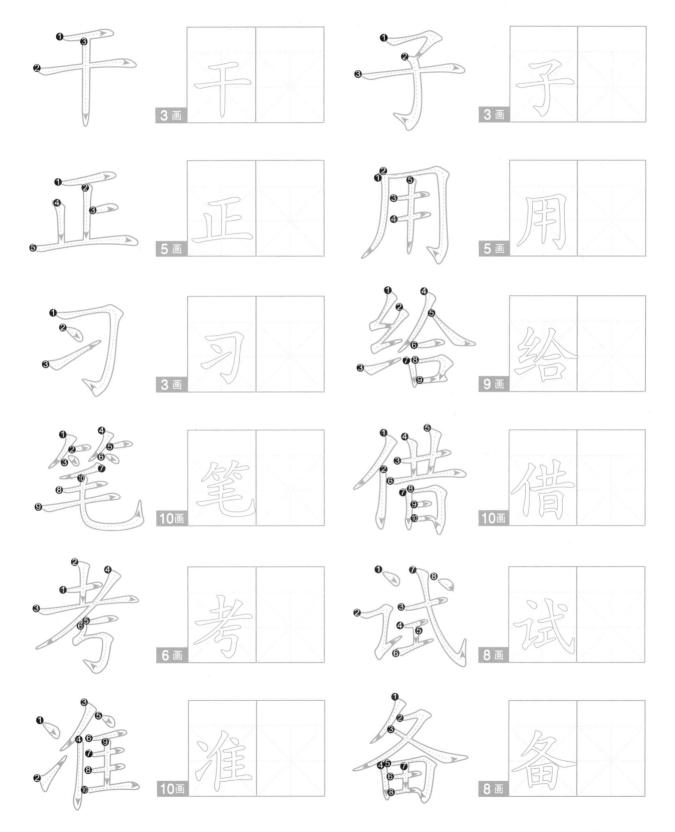

干　3画
子　3画
正　5画
用　5画
习　3画
给　9画
笔　10画
借　10画
考　6画
试　8画
准　10画
备　8画

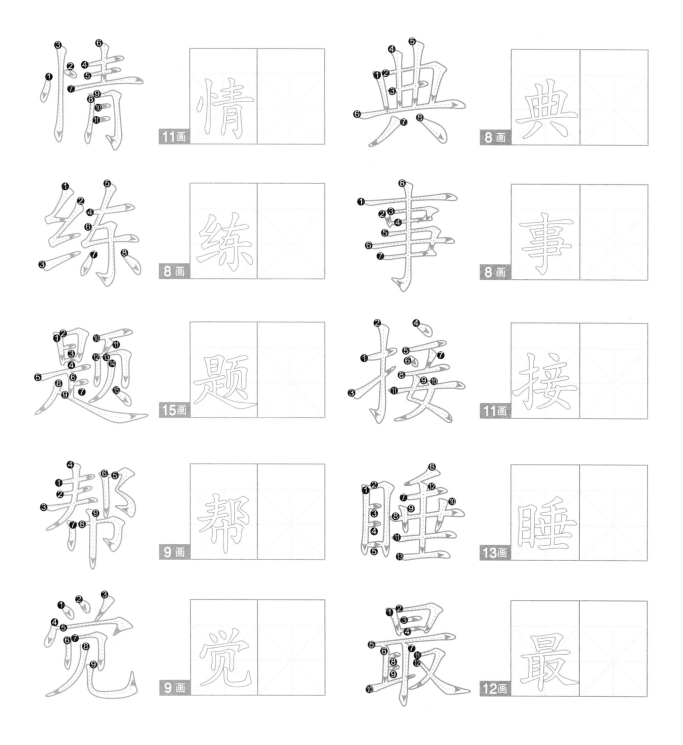

情 11画
典 8画
练 8画
事 8画
题 15画
接 11画
帮 9画
睡 13画
觉 9画
最 12画

19

第十九课　我刚买的电脑又便宜又好

Learning objectives

Learn how to use attributive clauses
Learn how to express indirect disagreement
Learn how to express the idea of "both ... and ..."

生词 New Words

电脑	diànnǎo	n	computer	脑 brain
感兴趣	gǎn xìngqu	v-o	be interested in	兴趣 interest 兴 pleased 趣 qù interest
生产	shēngchǎn	v	produce, make	产 produce
制造	zhìzào	v	make, manufacture	制 make 造 create, make
忘	wàng	v	forget	
听	tīng	v	listen, hear	
听课	tīngkè	v	listen to/attend a lecture	
手提	shǒutí	adj	portable	手 hand 提 pick up; lift
过时	guòshí	adj	dated, out of date	
认真	rènzhēn	adj	conscientious; earnest	
高兴	gāoxìng	adj	pleased	
进口	jìnkǒu	v	import	进 come in, move forward
牌子	páizi	n	brand (product)	牌 card, plaque
女孩儿	nǚháir	n	girl	孩 child
手机	shǒujī	n	mobile phone	机 machine
产品	chǎnpǐn	n	product	品 item, goods
礼物	lǐwù	n	gift, present	礼 ritual; courteous 物 thing, object
东西	dōngxi	n	thing, object	
美国	Měiguó	p.n	USA	
各	gè	pron	each	
种	zhǒng	m.w	kind, type	
台	tái	m.w	for machines	
又	yòu	conj/adv	again, once more	(又⋯又⋯ both ... and ...)
那儿	nàr	pron/l.w	there	
当时	dāngshí	n	at that time	当 just as, on the spot

句型 Speech Patterns

Modifier	的	S	是 O
		那个女孩 Nàge nǚhái	是我妹妹。 shì wǒ mèimei.
找我 Zhǎo wǒ	的 de	那个女孩 nàge nǚhái	是我妹妹。 shì wǒ mèimei.
昨天来找我 Zuótiān lái zhǎo wǒ	的 de	那个女孩 nàge nǚhái	是我妹妹。 shì wǒ mèimei.

An attributive clause in Chinese always precedes the word it modifies, linked by the attributive marker 的. If the word modified is the "doer" of the action in the attributive clause, the clause starts with the verb and its modifier (such as a time word) directly.

S 是	Modifier	的	O
这是 Zhè shì			电脑。 diànnǎo.
这是 Zhè shì	去年生产 qùnián shēngchǎn	的 de	电脑。 diànnǎo.
这是 中国 Zhè shì Zhōngguó	去年生产 qùnián shēngchǎn	的 de	电脑。 diànnǎo.

The word modified could be the "receiver" of the action in the attributive clause. In this case, the clause starts with the subject and verb of the clause, with its object following the attributive marker 的.

S	Adj	是 Adj,	就是	Adv Adj
这车 Zhè chē	好 hǎo	是好, shì hǎo,	就是 jiùshì	太贵了。 tài guì le.
这新电脑快 Zhè xīn diànnǎo kuài		是快, shì kuài,	就是 jiùshì	有点儿贵。 yóudiánr guì.
烤鸭 Kǎoyā	好吃 hǎochī	是好吃, shì hǎochī,	就是 jiùshì	不好做。 bú hǎo zuò.

This expression is usually used to bring up an unsatisfactory aspect of a seemingly good item, thus it is a rhetorical concession. 就是 can be replaced by 可是 in this pattern.

S	又	Adj	又	Adj
炒饭 Chǎofàn	又 yòu	便宜 piányi	又 yòu	好吃。 hǎochī.
我刚买的电脑 Wǒ gāng mǎi de diànnǎo	又 yòu	快 kuài	又 yòu	好。 hǎo.
他中文说得 Tā Zhōngwén shuō de	又 yòu	流利 liúlì	又 yòu	好听。 hǎotīng.

This construction can be used to link two verbs, adjectives or complements. The construction has a similar meaning to "既...又 ...".

补充词汇 Additional Vocabulary

跨国公司	kuàguó gōngsī	multinational firm		服装	fúzhuāng	garment
名牌产品	míngpái chǎnpǐn	brand name products		玩具	wánjù	toys
金融产品	jīnróng chǎnpǐn	financial products		家电	jiādiàn	household appliances
日用品	rìyòngpǐn	day to day products		冰箱	bīngxiāng	fridge
化妆品	huàzhuāngpǐn	cosmetic products		音响	yīnxiǎng	hi-fi
农产品	nóngchǎnpǐn	agricultural products		出口	chūkǒu	export

🔊 对话 1 Dialogue One

王京：小李，这就是你昨天刚买的电脑吗？

李东：对。这台电脑比我去年买的那台快多了。

王京：你是在哪儿买的？

李东：在学校旁边那家新开的商店里买的。

王京：那儿卖不卖手提电脑？

　　　我想给我女朋友买一个①。

李东：卖。那里有各种牌子的手提电脑。

王京：有没有进口的？

李东：有。有美国的、日本的……

王京：有没有中国生产的？

李东：有。你为什么对中国生产的电脑感兴趣②？

王京：因为我女朋友喜欢。她说中国制造的东西又便宜又好。

🔊 对话 2 Dialogue Two

王京：李东，昨天来找你的那个女孩儿是谁？

李东：是我妹妹。

王京：我还以为是你刚认识的女朋友呢。

李东：昨天上课时打电话给我的才是我女朋友③ & ④。

王京：当时大家都在认真听课，老师很不高兴。

李东：我知道，我忘了关机了。

王京：你用的是什么手机？我这个是去年刚买的，但已经过时了。

李东：我的是最新产品⑤。你看看。

王京：真漂亮。

李东：漂亮是漂亮，

　　　就是太贵了。

王京：你是花多少钱买的?

李东：这不是我买的，

　　　是我女朋友送给我的生日礼物。

语法注释 Grammar Notes

① **我想给我女朋友买一个** — 给 here means "for". The sentence pattern can be changed into "to buy something for someone".

> **For example:**
>
> 他爸爸给他买了一台新电脑。
> ——他爸爸买了一台新电脑给他。

② **你为什么对中国生产的电脑感兴趣?** — 对... 感兴趣 means "be interested in something". It could be changed into 对...有兴趣.

> **For example:**
>
> 老王对学习法语不感兴趣。
> ——老王对学习法语没有兴趣。

③ **昨天上课时** — This means "during yesterday's lesson" or "when we were having our lesson". The expression is a abbr. of 昨天上课的时侯.

④ **昨天上课时打电话给我的才是我女朋友** — 才 is here for emphasis. It means that the one Wang Jing mentioned is not my girl friend, but the one who called me yesterday is.

⑤ **最新产品** — 最 is a prefix of superlative degree.

> **For example:**
>
> a. 王京是我最好的朋友。
> b. 我最不喜欢喝啤酒。
> c. 他来得最晚。

文化知识 Cultural Note

现代中文里的词汇　Modern Chinese Vocabulary

Many words in modern Chinese are made up of two or three characters in order to accommodate the needs for new terminologies as a result of rapid social and technological developments. As Chinese uses existing characters to express new ideas and concepts, knowing the principal meanings of characters helps to understand the meaning of the new words made up of these characters. The meanings of some characters may extend over the years, such as 电, whose meaning has extended now to cover both electrical and electronics. The following are

examples of some words formed with 电: 电话, 电视, 电灯, 电机, 电表, 电工, 电流, 电笔, 电子, 电子表, 电子钟, 电脑.

练习 Exercises

口语练习 Speaking Practice

1. Working in pairs, tell your partner what you think of each of the following items using the vocabulary provided. Follow the following speech patterns.

1) 这本书好是好，就是太贵了。

2) 我的电脑又便宜又好。

电子	字典	好贵
中国生产的自行车	好	便宜
我朋友	会唱歌	会跳舞
这个东西	好看	没有用
我的电脑	新	贵
这家饭店的烤鸭	便宜	好吃

2. Imagine you bought two laptops or mobile phones. Make a comparison between the two using attributive clauses. For example, "The one I bought this year is faster, but more expensive than the one I bought last year...."

听力练习 Listening Practice

Listen to the recording, and circle the correct answer in each group, accordingly. Each dialogue or statement has one or two questions.

1) a. 中国   b. 美国   c. 英国

2) a. 中国   b. 美国   c. 英国

3) a. 很感兴趣   b. 有点儿兴趣   c. 不感兴趣

4) a. 给他太太写信   b. 学中文   c. 听音乐

5) a. 普通朋友   b. 男朋友   c. 哥哥

6) a. 很贵   b. 很便宜   c. 很漂亮

7) a. 他哥哥   b. 他爸爸   c. 他女朋友

8) a. 手机   b. 音乐光盘   c. 电脑

语法练习 Grammar Practice

1. Choose the correct position for 的 in the following sentences.

1) 我和我<u>A</u>姐姐昨天是坐<u>B</u>火车来<u>C</u>。 （　　　）

2) 他给他女<u>A</u>朋友买<u>B</u>新手机很好看<u>C</u>。 （　　　）

3) 那个<u>A</u>喜欢上网<u>B</u>学生叫什么<u>C</u>名字？ （　　　）

4) 我老师<u>A</u>爱人<u>B</u>弟弟是我<u>C</u>朋友。 （　　　）

5) 我们昨天去<u>A</u>那个<u>B</u>商店是个<u>C</u>美国商店。 （　　　）

6) 我没买我<u>A</u>朋友写<u>B</u>那本中文<u>C</u>小说。 （　　　）

2. Fill in the blanks of each of the following sentences using 一边 … 一边 … or 又 … 又 …

1) 她 ＿＿＿＿＿ 高＿＿＿＿＿ 瘦。

2) 我妈妈做的菜 ＿＿＿＿＿ 好吃， ＿＿＿＿＿ 好看。

3) 张先生总是 ＿＿＿＿＿ 喝酒， ＿＿＿＿＿ 看足球赛。

4) 我 ＿＿＿＿＿ 累 ＿＿＿＿＿ 渴。

5) 我喜欢 ＿＿＿＿＿ 看书， ＿＿＿＿＿ 听音乐。

6) 我们 ＿＿＿＿＿ 走， ＿＿＿＿＿ 唱吧。

3. Multiple choice.

1) 我的手机不是 ＿＿＿＿＿ 。

a. 名牌　　　　b. 有名　　　　c. 牌子

2) 我要 ＿＿＿＿＿ 我妈妈买一台电视。

a. 想　　　　b. 到　　　　c. 给

3) 昨天晚上睡觉前，我 ＿＿＿＿＿ 了吃药了。

a. 忘　　　　b. 想　　　　c. 没忘

4) 你 ＿＿＿＿＿ 明天几点考试吗？

a. 认识　　　　b. 说　　　　c. 知道

5) 我去年刚买的电脑现在已经 ＿＿＿＿＿ 了。

a. 过时　　　　b. 过去　　　　c. 不过

6) 你是法国人！我还 ＿＿＿＿＿ 你是英国人呢。

a. 认为　　　　b. 以为　　　　c. 知道

认字识词 Words with Known Characters

Figure out the English meanings of each of the words below and write them in the spaces provided.

前进	_____	进来	_____
礼品	_____	产地	_____
人造	_____	手工	_____
车牌	_____	王牌	_____
生手	_____	孩子	_____
趣事	_____	提高	_____

翻译练习 Translation

Say the following sentences in Chinese first, then write them out in characters.

1) The roast duck his father cooked yesterday was really delicious.

2) Do you know the girl over there who is speaking with our teacher?

3) This is the birthday present that my boyfriend gave me last year.

4) That is a new product, it is very good and very cheap.

5) This mobile is very pretty, but it is not the newest model, it is a bit dated.

6) The person who sells fruit outside the train station is my friend's father.

阅读 Reading

伦敦的中文书店

伦敦有很多卖中文书的书店。要是你想买中文书，你可以去中国城 (Chinatown) 买，那里有两三家中文书店。你也可以去普通大书店买，现在很多英国书店都开始卖中文书了。不过，伦敦还有一家专门 (specialised) 卖中文图书的公司 (company)。这家公司很大，里面有很多中文书和中文光盘。

这家公司是中国图书总公司 (parent company) 的伦敦分公司 (subsidiary)。

公司离地铁站和公共汽车站都不远。公司里的中文书有汉语口语、汉语写作、汉语语法、中国文学和书法等等。这些书大多是北京大学、北京语言大学的老师写的。公司还有很多中国音乐和中国电影光盘。有时间你可以去看看，一定能买到你喜欢的东西。

Please answer the following questions based on the information in the above text.

1) Where can one buy Chinese books in London now?

2) Did many British bookstores sell Chinese books before now?

3) What is the London based company that specialises in selling Chinese books?

4) What kind of books does this company sell?

5) What kinds of CDs and DVDs can one get from this company?

汉字知识 Chinese Characters

偏旁 Radicals

The semantic associations of three radicals are given in the table below. Can you work out and write their related characters according to the pinyin provided?

刂	knife	gāng	kè	zhì	
纟	silk	hóng	lǜ	gěi	jīng
夕	sunset	suì	duō	míng	wài

汉字笔顺 Stroke Order

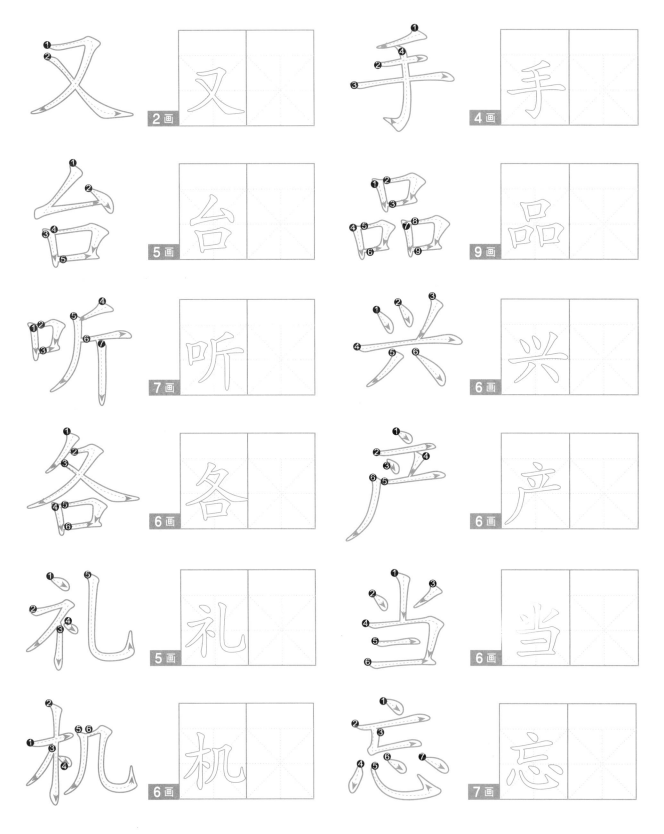

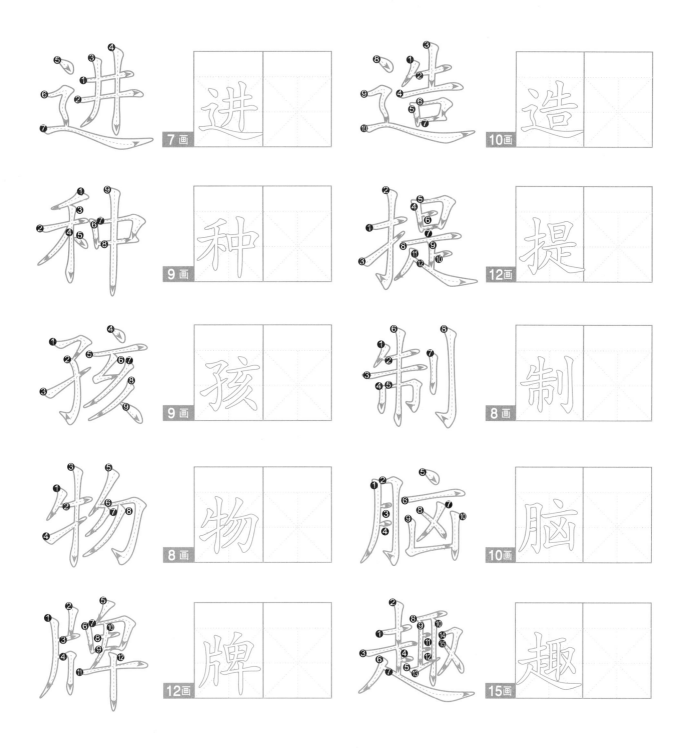

20

第二十课　　你去过长城吗?

Learning objectives

Learn how to talk about an imminent future action
Learn how to talk about past experiences
Learn how to talk about two consecutive actions in sequence

生词 New Words

打算	dǎsuàn	v/n	plan	算 calculate
放假	fàngjià	v-o	be on vacation	放 release; put　假 holiday, leave
度假	dùjià	v-o	go on vacation	度 pass, spend
玩儿	wánr	v	play; have fun	
听说	tīngshuō	v	it is said; people say	
可爱	kě'ài	adj	lovely	
大熊猫	dàxióngmāo	n	panda	熊 bear
动物园	dòngwùyuán	n	zoo	动物 animal　　动 move
飞机票	fēijīpiào	n	plane ticket	飞机 plane　　飞 fly
国家	guójiā	n	country, nation state	
大陆	dàlù	n	continent	陆 land; land mass
欧洲	Ōuzhōu	p.n	Europe	洲 continent
德国	Déguó	p.n	Germany	德 Germany (abbr.); virtue
意大利	Yìdàlì	p.n	Italy	意 Italy (abbr.); meaning; intention
比利时	Bǐlìshí	p.n	Belgium	
西班牙	Xībānyá	p.n	Spain	牙 tooth
长城	Chángchéng	p.n	Great Wall	城 city; wall
长江	Chángjiāng	p.n	Yangtze River	江 large river
黄山	Huáng Shān	p.n	Huangshan Mountain	黄 yellow　山 mountain
黄河	Huánghé	p.n	Yellow River	河 river
云南	Yúnnán	p.n	Yunnan (province)	云 cloud
四川	Sìchuān	p.n	Sichuan (province)	川 Sichuan; flat river or land
海南	Hǎinán	p.n	Hainan (province)	
马上	mǎshàng	adv	right away	马 horse
当然	dāngrán	adv	of course, certainly	
些*	xiē	n	some	

句型 Speech Patterns

S	要	V	O	了
我 Wǒ	要 yào	去 qù	北京 Běijīng	了。 le.
我 Wǒ	就要 jiùyào	去 qù	北京 Běijīng	了。 le.
我 Wǒ	快要 kuàiyào	去 qù	北京 Běijīng	了。 le.

The expression (快/就)要 ... 了 indicates an imminent action, which suggests a change of status from that at the time of speaking.

S	Adv	V 过	O
他 Tā		去过 qùguò	中国。 Zhōngguó.
他 Tā	没 méi	去过 qùguò	美国。 Měiguó.
他 Tā	从来没 cónglái méi	吃过 chīguò	烤鸭。 kǎoyā.

过 indicates a past experience. It is normally used with an unspecific time. As it refers to actions that took place in the past, it is negated with 没.

S	TW	V1 了	O1	V2 O2
老李 Lǎo Lǐ	天天 tiāntiān	吃了 chīle	晚饭 wǎnfàn	就喝茶。 jiù hēchá.
我们 Wǒmen		去了 qùle	法国 Fǎguó	去德国。 qù Déguó.
她 Tā	昨天 zuótiān	喝了 hēle	啤酒 píjiǔ	喝红酒。 hē hóngjiǔ.

The suffix 了 indicates the completion of an action before another action takes place. The pair of actions could take place in the future, in the habitual present, or in the past.

S1	一	V1 O1	S2	就	V2	O2
学校 Xuéxiào	一 yí	放假, fàngjià,	我 wǒ	就 jiù	走。 zǒu.	
老师 Lǎoshī	一 yì	来, lái,	我们 wǒmen	就 jiù	上 shàng	课。 kè.
我 Wǒ	一 yí	下班, xiàbān,		就 jiù	回 huí	家。 jiā.

一 ... 就 is used to imply that a second action will happen as soon as a first action takes place. 一 emphasises "as soon as" while 就 stresses the immediateness of the second action.

补充词汇 Additional Vocabulary

名胜古迹	míngshèng-gǔjì	places of interest		游艇	yóutǐng	yacht
景点	jǐngdiǎn	scenic spot		观光	guānguāng	sightseeing
旅游团	lǚyóutuán	tourist group		购物	gòuwù	shopping
旅游车	lǚyóuchē	tour coach		导游	dǎoyóu	tour guide
旅游船	lǚyóuchuán	cruise ship		爬山	páshān	mountain climbing
旅行社	lǚxíngshè	travel agency		潜水	qiánshuǐ	diving

对话 1 Dialogue One

小李：小黄，马上就要放假了，你打算去哪儿玩儿？

小黄：我打算去中国的海南。听说那里美极了。

小李：美是美，就是太远了。

小黄：你打算去哪儿度假？

小李：去欧洲大陆。

小黄：你从来没有去过欧洲大陆吗？

小李：去是去过，可是没有好好玩儿过。

小黄：这次你打算去哪些国家？

小李：我想先去比利时，去了比利时去德国。

小黄：去了德国去意大利？

小李：我以前去过意大利了，这次去了德国去西班牙。

🔊 对话 2 Dialogue Two

小李：小王，听说你要去中国。

小王：对，我以前从来没去过①&②。你去过没有？

小李：去过好多次了③。

小王：长城、长江你去过没有？

小李：去过。

小王：黄山、黄河你也去过了吗？

小李：当然去过了。中国有名的地方我差不多都去过了。

小王：听说云南很美。

小李：去过的人都说很美。

小王：这次我想先去云南，去了云南再去四川看大熊猫。

小李：大熊猫可爱极了。你没见过大熊猫吗？

小王：我只在动物园里见过。

小李：你打算什么时候走？

小王：飞机票我都买了④，一放假我就走。

语法注释 Grammar Notes

① 过 and 了— 过 indicates a past "experience" while 了 suggests the completion of an action or a change of status as a result of an action. Compare the following two pairs of sentences to see the difference between these characters:

> **Compare:**
>
> **a.** 1) 我学过两年中文。I have previonsly studied Chinese for two years (prior to the time of speaking but possibly at any time in the past).
>
> 2) 我学了两年中文了。I have studied Chinese for two years now (by the time of speaking the speaker could he continuing or have just finished studying).
>
> **b.** 1) 他去过北京。He has been to Beijing before (he could be anywhere now).
>
> 2) 他去北京了。He has gone to Beijing (he is in Beijing now).

② 我以前从来没去过— 从来没 indicates that an action has never taken place, while 从来不 indicate a frequent or habitual action. Please note the differences between them in the following sentences:

他从来不喝啤酒。   He never drinks beer.

他从来没喝过中国啤酒。   He has never drunk Chinese beer before.

③ 去过好多次了 — This sentence means, "I have been there quite a few times". 好多 is similar to 很多 and 次 is a measure word for an action verb.

④ 飞机票我都买了—都 means "already".

> **For example:**
>
> 那本书我都看了三遍了.

文化知识 Cultural Note

长城和黄河

The Great Wall and the Yellow River

The Great Wall and the Yellow River are often regarded as symbols of China and Chinese culture. The Great Wall is a man-made wonder, extending over 5,000 kilometres from northeast to northwest. The Yellow River has a unique role in Chinese culture, not only because the River nurtured early agricultural communities, but also because according to Chinese legend, one of the earliest Chinese ancestors, the Yellow Emperor (黄帝— Huángdì) lived along the River. That is why the Yellow River is referred fo as the birthplace of the Chinese civilisation.

练习 Exercises

口语练习 Speaking Practice

Working in pairs, talk about your travel plans for the coming summer using the speech patterns from this lesson.

时间	去哪儿	和谁去	怎么去
七月	黄山, 长江, 上海	三个朋友	飞机, 火车
下个月	法国, 意大利	女/男朋友	开车
放假以后	回家, 西班牙	一个人	火车, 地铁
从8月25日到9月10日	北京, 四川, 云南	商学院同学	飞机, 火车, 自行车

听力练习 Listening Practice

Listen to the recording, and circle the correct answer in each group, accordingly. Each dialogue or statement has two questions.

1) a. 去过   b. 没去过   c. 马上去
2) a. 长城很长   b. 长城很有名   c. 长城很新
3) a. 这个星期   b. 下个月   c. 下个星期
4) a. 意大利   b. 比利时   c. 德国
5) a. 去看北京   b. 去看长城   c. 去看熊猫

6)　a. 机票太贵　　b. 没有时间　　c. 中国太远

7)　a. 有很多博物馆　b. 天气不很好　　c. 很漂亮

8)　a. 春天和夏天　　b. 夏天和秋天　　c. 秋天和冬天

语法练习 Grammar Practice

1. Please fill in the blanks with 了 or 过.

1)　昨天他坐飞机去北京 _____。

2)　他从来没坐 _____ 飞机。

3)　我已经学了六个月的中文 _____。

4)　你来晚了，餐厅已经关门 _____。

5)　我吃 _____ 中国炒面，好吃极 _____。

6)　我以前从来没去 _____ 王老师家，昨天去 _____。
他家又大又漂亮。

7)　这个问题你以前想 _____ 没有？

8)　他喝 _____ 九瓶啤酒了，不能再喝了。

2. Arrange the words in the correct order to make sentences.

1)　法语　两年　我　　了　　学　了

2)　去　　上海　海南　李老师　了　去　打算

3)　中国　你　去　　他　　过　没　知道　去　？

4)　美　　他们　最　　黄山　说

5)　北京　我们　马上　了　　就　到　要

6)　小说　他　看　写　　的　没　从来　我　过

认字识词 Words with Known Characters

Figure out the English meanings of each of the words below and write them in the spaces provided.

听写 _____　　北极熊 _____

放学	_____	骑马	_____
赛马	_____	马路	_____
山路	_____	山水	_____
亚洲	_____	非洲	_____
北美洲	_____	南美洲	_____

翻译练习 Translation

Say the following sentences in Chinese first, then write them out in characters.

1) The train will depart soon, please board the train immediately.

2) Miss Huang will go to China as soon as the school holiday starts.

3) My younger sister said that the panda is the loveliest of all animals.

4) My father has been to Shanghai, but he has never been to Beijing.

5) I haven't drank Chinese beer before, but I shall have a glass of it today.

6) They are soon going to continental Europe for a holiday.

阅读 Reading

我的第一次中国旅行

去过中国的人都知道中国很大，好玩儿的地方也很多。我从小就对中国感兴趣，可是一直没有机会 (chance) 去。去年夏天机会来了，我的好朋友马克 (Mark) 那时 (at that time) 正在中国学习汉语，他请我去中国度假，我高兴极了。这是我第一次去中国。

我是先到的北京。马克那时还没有放假，我就一个人先去看了长城。长城又高又长，非常漂亮。学校一放假，马克和我就去了西安 (Xi'an)。我们去了西安去山东，去了山东去上海，去了上海又去黄山。七月的中国，天气很热，虽然黄山很美，可是我们没有好好看。从黄山一下来，我们就去了海南。海南真是漂亮极了。我们玩得非常高兴。我对马克说，这次没有好好看黄山，明年我一定再来。

Please answer the following questions based on the information in the above text.

1) When did the writer become interested in China?

2) Why did the writer choose to go to China last summer?

3) What places did they visit in China?

4) What was the weather like in China at that time?

5) What is the writer's plan for the next year?

 ## 汉字知识 Chinese Characters

偏旁 Radicals

The semantic associations of three radicals are given in the table below. Can you work out and write their related characters according to the pinyin provided?

⺮	bamboo	dì	lán	suàn	děng	bǐ
阝	mound (on the left), town (on the right)	lù	yuàn	jiàng	dū/dōu	nà
灬	fire	diǎn	rè	rán	xióng	

汉字笔顺 Stroke Order

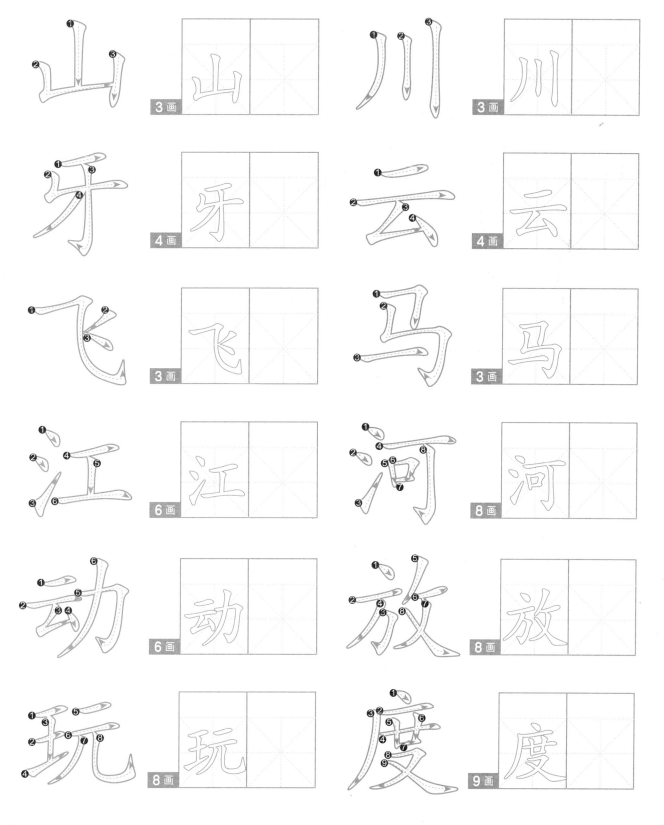

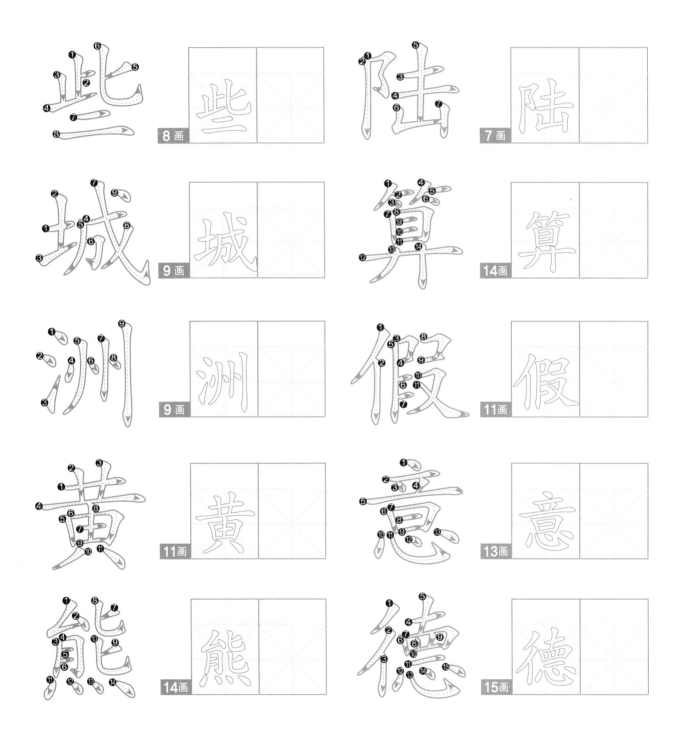

附录一　Appendix 1

常用偏旁　Common Radicals

部首 Radical	语义 Meaning	名称 Description in Chinese	例字 Example
冫	ice	两点水	冰
刂	knife	立刀旁	到
讠	speech, word	言字旁	语
亻	single person	单立人	你
阝	mound, town	耳刀旁	都
廴	structure	建字旁	建
厂	factory	偏厂儿	斤
冖	roof	秃宝盖	写
勹	bag	包字头	句
厶	private	私字儿	么
氵	water	三点水	法
艹	grass	草字头	英
扌	hand	提手旁	打
辶	walk quickly	走之旁	这
忄	heart	竖心旁	忙
宀	roof	宝盖头	客
彡	ornament	斜三撇	须
饣	food	食字旁	饭
犭	animal	反犬旁	猫
业	small	小字头	光
彳	step out	双立人	很
囗	enclosure	大口框	国
纟	silk	绞丝旁	纪
牜	cattle	牛字旁	牲
灬	fire	四点底	热
礻	show	示补旁	被
钅	metal	金字旁	铁
疒	illness	病字旁	瘦
攵	hand holding a stick	反文旁	敦
穴	hole	穴宝盖	空
衤	clothing	衣补旁	补
卢	tiger	虎字头	虎
𧾷	foot	足字旁	踢
人	person	人字头	今
孑	child	子字旁	孩
白	white	白字旁	的
又	right hand	又字旁	对
力	strength	力字底	男
土	soil, earth	提土旁	地
弓	bow	弓字旁	张

部首 Radical	语义 Meaning	名称 Description in Chinese	例字 Example
广	wide, vast	广字旁	庆
口	mouth	口字旁	吗
夕	sunset	夕字旁	名
门	door	门字框	闲
工	work	工字旁	功
女	woman	女字旁	好
巾	cloth, towel	巾字旁	帽
尸	corpse	尸字头	屋
山	mountain	山字旁	峨
马	horse	马字旁	骑
王	king; jade	王字旁	环
日	sun	日字旁	明
月	moon; flesh	月字旁	期
气	air	气字头	氛
心	heart	心字底	您
户	single door	户字头	房
车	vehicle	车字旁	辆
父	father	父字头	爸
贝	seashell	贝字底	贵
方	square	方字旁	放
火	fire	火字旁	烤
木	wood, tree	木字旁	林
石	stone, rock	石字旁	碗
目	eye	目字底	看
田	field	田字头	累
皿	container, utensil	皿字底	盘
禾	cereal	禾木旁	利
鸟	bird	鸟字旁	鸭
立	stand	立字旁	站
耳	ear	耳字旁	聪
虫	insect	虫字旁	蛤
竹	bamboo	竹字头	篮
舟	boat	舟字旁	船
米	rice	米字旁	籽
身	body	身字旁	射
雨	rain	雨字头	雪
鱼	fish	鱼字旁	鲜
革	leather	革字旁	鞋
酉	container	酉字旁	醒

附录二　Appendix 2

组词游戏　Word Game

How many Chinese words and phrases can you find in the following table? They are formed only with the neighbouring characters, but characters can be used more than once, and the formation can be in any direction, up down, left right (or vice versa), and diagonally.

品	产	灯	始	关	火	发	烧	斤	公
牌	绿	花	开	放	进	毛	动	物	园
红	黄	河	门	口	笔	病	生	矿	睡
度	山	东	江	试	考	果	泉	觉	感
假	期	城	长	向	药	水	对	得	馆
币	舞	跳	远	近	方	便	面	使	用
国	民	好	歌	高	前	话	大	上	海
间	爱	人	手	提	电	脑	孩	边	马
时	有	情	书	出	路	子	怪	女	院
坏	事	没	本	金	找	错	字	学	校
快	车	票	换	钱	现	常	非	典	礼
手	机	分	支	交	通	利	洲	亚	中
飞	过	钟	头	行	流	南	美	欧	餐
来	后	路	银	外	旅	北	京	元	西

附录三 Appendix 3

听力原文 Listening Scripts

Lesson 11

听力练习 Listening Practice

Listen to the short dialogues and circle the correct answer in each group, accordingly.

1. 男：请问，大英图书馆在哪儿？
   女：就在前面。
2. 男：小李，王老师在哪儿？
   女：他就在你后面。
3. 男：请问，东方商店在哪儿？
   女：在银行东边。
4. 男：地铁站在公园的东面还是西面？
   女：地铁站在公园的西面。
5. 男：李小英旁边的那个人是谁？
   女：那是李老师，他是我们的中文老师。
6. 男：这儿有火车吗？
   女：没有，这儿只有地铁。
7. 男：王先生在哪儿？
   女：他在外面的汽车里边。
8. 男：你怎么去大学商学院？
   女：我开车去。

Lesson 12

听力练习 Listening Practice

Listen to the short dialogues and circle the correct answer in each group, accordingly.

1. 男：请问，可乐多少钱一瓶？
   女：小的两块五一瓶，大的四块一瓶。
   问题：How much is it for a small bottle?
2. 女：你们有没有北京的明信片？
   男：有。你要几张？
   女：我要四张。
   问题：How many postcards is she going to buy?
3. 男：请问，一共多少钱？
   女：一共四十二块。
   男：这是五十块。
   问题：How much did he give her?
4. 男：您好！您想买点儿什么？
   女：请问有没有中国音乐光盘？

男：对不起。我们这儿只有西方音乐光盘。

问题：What kind of music CDs does the shop have?

5. 女：十块钱一张光盘太贵了，能不能便宜点儿？

男：你多买点儿，八块一张，怎么样？

女：好，我买五张。

问题：How many is she going to buy?

6. 女：汉语口语书多少钱一本？

男：25块钱一本。

女：我买两本。

问题：How much is it altogether?

7. 女：请问明信片怎么卖？

男：两块钱一张。买一送一。

女：我要十张。

问题：How much will she pay?

8. 男：小李，这家法国饭馆太贵了！我们去那家中国饭馆吧。

女：可是那家中国饭馆也不便宜。

男：比这家法国饭馆便宜。

问题：Why are they going to the Chinese restaurant?

Lesson 13

听力练习　Listening Practice

1. Listen to the recording and fill in the correct times on the clocks.

Picture 1: 我早上七点一刻吃早饭。

Picture 2: 我差五分九点开始上课。

Picture 3: 我下午两点喝茶。

Picture 4: 我晚上七点上网学汉语。

2. Listen to the short dialogues and circle the correct answer in each group, accordingly.

1) 女：请问，现在几点了？

男：十点四十。

2) 女：请问，学校餐厅几点开门？

男：早上七点半开门。

3) 女：水果店什么时候关门？

男：水果店晚上十一点半关门。

4) 女：苹果多少钱一斤？

男：苹果七块九一斤。

5) 女：小王，你们几点开始上课？

男：差一刻九点。

6) 女：现在几点？

男：现在下午三点。

7) 女：星期六图书馆开不开门？

男：开门，上午十点半开门。

8) 男：学校晚上几点关门？

女：十一点半关门。

Lesson 14

听力练习　Listening Practice

Listen to the short dialogues and circle the correct answer in each group, accordingly.

1. 男：李英，你去哪儿？
   女：我去第二十一中学。
2. 男：你有点儿感冒。打一针，好吗？
   女：医生，我不要打针，我想吃西药。
3. 男：请问，去大英图书馆坐几路公共汽车？
   女：你可以坐44路公共汽车。
4. 男：请问，从这儿到火车站走路要几分钟？
   女：走路要半个小时。
5. 男：从你家到学校要几分钟？
   女：坐地铁要一刻钟，坐公共汽车要半个小时，骑车要三刻钟。
6. 男：这药怎么吃？
   女：一日两次，一次三片。
7. 男：请问，去商学院怎么走？
   女：到十字路口向左拐。
8. 男：医生，这药应该饭前吃还是饭后吃？
   女：这药应该六小时吃一次，一次两片。

Lesson 15

听力练习　Listening Practice

Listen to the short dialogues and circle the correct answer in each group, accordingly.

1. 男：我昨天去看病了。我感冒了。
   女：你吃药了吗？现在怎么样了？
   男：吃了。现在好多了。
   问题：What treatment did the man receive for his cold?
2. 女：小王，你比以前胖了？
   男：是胖了，我比以前胖了五公斤。
   问题：How much weight did Xiao Wang put on?
3. 女：老李,你星期六晚上还去打太极拳吗？
   男：不打了。我开始打网球了。
   问题：What sports does the man do now?
4. 男：一美元能换多少人民币？
   女：美元现在下跌了。只能换六块三了。
   问题：Which of the following might have been the exchange rate previous to today?
5. 男：你好,你们收不收旅行支票？
   女：收，我们既收旅行支票，也收现金。
   男：太好了。我有美元旅行支票，想换点儿欧元。
   问题：What currency was the man interested in purchasing?
6. 男：李英，你累不累？
   女：我不累，我饿。
   男：你今天吃早饭了没有？

女：没有。

问题：Why was Li Ying so hungry?

7. 男：五百英镑可以换多少人民币？

女：今天可以换五千一百元。

问题：How many yuan can 500 pounds be exchanged for today?

8. 男：小李，你瘦了。

女：我是瘦了一点儿。我以前太胖了。

问题：What did the lady reply?

Lesson 16

听力练习　Listening Practice

Listen to the short dialogues and circle the correct answer in each group, accordingly. Each dialogue has two questions.

1. 男：对不起我来晚了。我的自行车坏了，我是走路来的。走了一个多小时。

女：没关系。我也是刚到。

问题1：他是怎么来的？

问题2：他走了多长时间？

2. 女：你家离学校远吗？

男：不远也不近。

女：通常你都怎么来学校？

男：我坐地铁来。坐公共汽车要二十多分钟。

问题3：从他家到学校坐公共汽车要多长时间？

问题4：他通常怎么来学校？

3. 女：你星期六和星期天都做什么？

男：我很爱看足球，所以星期六和星期天我常常看足球比赛。

女：昨天英国和法国的球赛你看了没有？

男：没看。我家的电视坏了。

问题5：他星期六、星期天都做什么？

问题6：他昨天为什么没有看足球比赛？

4. 女：小方，你女朋友好吗？

男：我现在没有女朋友了。

女：她为什么离开你了？

男：她问我爱我的狗还是爱她？

女：你说爱狗。

男：不，我说都爱。

问题7：他对他女朋友说了什么？

问题8：他女朋友为什么离开他了？

Lesson 17

听力练习　Listening Practice

Listen to the short dialogues and circle the correct answer in each group, accordingly. Each dialogue has two or three questions.

1. 男：小英，昨天晚上你去哪儿了？

女：我去学校了。我们学校开中国新年晚会。

男：你也表演了吗? 你不是很喜欢唱歌吗?

女：我没有唱歌，我唱得不好。我和几个英国学生表演了中国功夫。

问题1：学校开的是什么晚会?

问题2：晚会是什么时候开的?

问题3：小英昨天表演了什么?

2. 女：我喜欢唱歌，可是我不会唱中文歌。你会唱中文歌吗?

男：我也不会，我只会打太极拳。

女：你知道谁会唱中文歌吗?

男：商学院的王先生会，图书馆的李小姐也会。

问题4：女的喜欢做什么?

问题5：男的会做什么?

问题6：王先生在哪儿上班?

3. 男：我女朋友是中国人, 她喜欢唱歌, 也喜欢跳舞。

女：她歌唱得怎么样? 舞跳得怎么样?

男：她歌唱得很不错。舞跳得不怎么样。

女：她是做什么的?

男：她是法学院的学生。

问题7：他女朋友歌唱得怎么样?

问题8：她在哪儿上学?

Lesson 18

听力练习　Listening Practice

Listen to the short dialogues, and circle the correct answer in each group, accordingly. Each dialogue has two or three questions.

1. 男：小李, 你的中文比我的好, 能不能帮我看看这张明信片?

女：行啊。你朋友说他新年要来英国看你。

男：谢谢你。我认识的汉字太少了, 我不认识这个"新"字。

问题1：他的朋友什么时候来英国?

问题2：他为什么让小李帮他看明信片?

2. 女：王京, 你最近在忙什么呢?

男：我在准备汉语考试。

女：什么时候考?

男：下个星期四。

女：你准备得怎么样了?

男：口试我应该没问题, 笔试还不行, 很多汉字我都不会写。

问题3：王京在忙什么?

问题4：什么时候考试?

问题5：王京为什么说他笔试不行?

3. 女：你昨晚打电话给我的时候, 我正在上班, 所以不能接电话。

男：没关系。你一边上学, 一边打工, 你累不累?

女：不累。我一个星期只干两个晚上。

男：下个星期的考试你准备得怎么样了?

女：我还没有准备。

问题6：她为什么没接电话？

问题7：她一个星期干几天？

问题8：下个星期的考试她准备得怎么样了？

Lesson 19

听力练习　Listening Practice

Listen to the recording, and circle the correct answer in each group, accordingly. Each dialogue or statement has one or two questions.

1. 男：小方，你这台手提电脑是在英国买的吗？

　女：不是，上个月我去美国看我男朋友，是在那儿买的。

　男：这是美国生产的吧？

　女：不是，这是中国生产的，又便宜又好。

　问题1：她的电脑是在哪儿买的？

　问题2：电脑是哪国生产的？

2. 女：老李，你怎么现在也对电脑感兴趣了？

　男：我太太去中国工作了，我想学电脑上网给她写信。

　问题3：老李以前对电脑有没有兴趣？

　问题4：老李现在为什么学电脑？

3. 男：你不要生气，刚才给我打电话的人，我真的不认识！

　女：不认识？不认识她怎么说她爱你？

　问题5：那个男的是女的什么人？

4. 女：你的手机真漂亮。

　男：漂亮是漂亮，可是不是最新产品。

　女：真的？我看看可以吗？

　男：给你，看吧。

　女：真漂亮。你是花多少钱买的？

　男：这是我哥哥给我的。他又换了一个新的。

　问题6：男的手机怎么样？

　问题7：男的手机是谁给的？

5. 女：明天是我弟弟十九岁的生日。我要送给他一个礼物。他很喜欢听
音乐，我准备送给他一张音乐光盘。

　问题8：她准备送给她弟弟一个什么礼物？

Lesson 20

听力练习　Listening Practice

Listen to the recording, and circle the correct answer in each group, accordingly. Each dialogue or statement has two questions.

1. 女：李贵，你去过中国没有？

　男：去过。

　女：你去过长城吗？

　男：当然去过。去过中国的人差不多都去过长城。

　问题1：李贵去过中国吗？

　问题2：李贵为什么说去过中国的人差不多都去过长城？

2. 女： 学校下个星期就要放假了，你打算去哪儿玩儿?
   男： 我打算跟朋友去欧洲玩儿。
   女： 欧洲有不少国家，你们准备去哪些国家?
   男： 这次我们准备去两个国家。先去法国，去了法国去比利时。
   问题3： 学校什么时候放假?
   问题4： 他打算去了法国去哪个国家?

3. 女： 我很喜欢动物，一直想去中国看看大熊猫。可是中国太远了，去中国的机票贵极了，所以我一直没有去。
   问题5： 她为什么想去中国?
   问题6： 她为什么还没有去?

4. 男： 伦敦城里公园很多，博物馆也很多。夏天和秋天的时候，总是有很多外国人来伦敦玩儿，因为那个时候，伦敦的天气最好，不冷不热。
   问题7： 为什么很多外国人喜欢来伦敦玩儿?
   问题8： 什么时候来伦敦玩儿最好?

附录四 Appendix 4

练习答案 Keys to the Exercises

Warm-up Lesson

填空 Fill in the blanks: Complete the following sentences by filling in the blanks with the appropriate words from the list below.

1) 我们要三<u>杯</u>牛奶。
2) 我<u>天天</u>晚上都看电视。
3) 北京夏天比伦敦<u>热</u>。
4) 你家有<u>几</u>口人？我家有五口人。
5) 你喜欢吃中国饭<u>还是</u>英国饭？
6) 我今天很忙，你忙<u>不</u>忙？
7) 我<u>没</u>有姐姐，可是有一个妹妹。
8) 今天是十<u>月</u>六号，星期二。
9) 她明天<u>坐</u>火车去伦敦看她男朋友。
10) 我爸爸喜欢吃中国饭，<u>喝</u>中国茶。

组句 Arrange the words in the correct order to make sentences.

1) 我们都是英国人。
2) 他们今天坐地铁去图书馆还书。
3) 王小姐很喜欢打网球。
4) 我们的中文老师是北京人。
5) 北京冬天比伦敦冷。
6) 他天天晚上写汉字。
7) 我妈妈不会做烤鸭/红烧肉，可是会做红烧肉/烤鸭。
8) 英国人应不应该学外语？
9) 我女朋友的狗/猫比我的猫/狗胖。
10) 明天是我哥哥的生日。

提问 Use question words to ask questions about the underlined parts of the following sentences.

1) 她叫<u>什么名字</u>？
2) <u>谁</u>是伦敦人？
3) 他们都是<u>哪国</u>人？
4) <u>哪天</u>是王京的生日？
5) 你妹妹今年<u>几</u>岁？
6) 下个星期天是<u>几</u>号？
7) 你今年<u>多大</u>？
8) 今天星期<u>几</u>？
9) 你女朋友想去<u>哪儿/什么地方</u>学汉语？
10) 你爸爸天天<u>怎么</u>去上班？

翻译练习　Translation

1) 你姓什么？我姓王。
2) 他是哪国人？他是中国人。
3) 今天几号？2012年2月19号。今天是我男朋友的生日。
4) 他天天晚上都看电视。
5) 我会说一点儿汉语，你呢？
6) 你有英文书吗？
7) 这个大学有很多学生。
8) 我弟弟比我小5岁，可是他比我高。
9) 你今天怎么去大学图书馆？坐公共汽车去。
10) 我哥哥是医生，他女朋友是律师。

Lesson 11

听力练习　Listening Practice

Listen to the short dialogues and circle the correct answer in each group, accordingly.

　　1) a　　　2) c　　　3) c　　　4) b　　　5) b　　　6) a　　　7) c　　　8) b

语法练习　Grammar Practice

1. Multiple choice.

　　1) a　　　2) b　　　3) b　　　4) a　　　5) c　　　6) b

2. Re-write the following sentences by swapping the subjects. The first sentence has been done as an example.

2) 公园在医院的前边。
3) 银行右边是大使馆。
4) 大英图书馆不在商学院南边。
5) 我在王小明的右边，在他太太的左边。/我在王小明和他太太的中间。
6) 中国在日本的西南边。

认字识词　Words with Known Characters

Figure out the English meanings of each of the words below and write them in the spaces provided.

外国	foreign	国外	overseas
上车	get on	下车	get off
下班	finish work	酒馆	pub
茶馆	tea house	饭馆	restaurant
南非	South Africa	东南亚	Southeast Asia
天使	angel	外星人	people from other planets, extraterrestrial beings

翻译练习　Translation

Say the following sentences in Chinese first, and then write them out in characters.

1) 图书馆在你家南面吗？不，图书馆在我家北面。
2) 火车站在银行对面。
3) 我们学院外面有两个商店。
4) 书店在图书馆和银行中间。
5) 中国大使馆在公园的旁边。
6) 李先生在外面的车里(面)。

Lesson 12
听力练习　Listening Practice
Listen to the short dialogues and circle the correct answer in each groups, accordingly.

　　1) b　　　　2) a　　　　3) c　　　　4) c　　　　5) b　　　　6) b　　　　7) c　　　　8) a

语法练习　Grammar Practice

1. Multiple choice.

　　1) a　　　　2) b　　　　3) c　　　　4) b　　　　5) b　　　　6) c

2. Choose the right question or answer to fill in each blank in the following dialogues. The first one has been is done as an example.

　　2) d　　　　3) c　　　　4) b　　　　5) e　　　　6) f

认字识词　Words with Known Characters

Figure out the English meanings of each of the words below and write them in the spaces provided.

口语	spoken language	语法	grammar
写信	write a letter	写作	composing/writing
名片	name card	图片	picture/photograph
泉水	spring water	暖水瓶	thermos bottle/flask
共和国	republic	买卖	business/trade
前方	front line	后方	rear base

翻译练习　Translation

Say the following sentences in Chinese first, and then write them out in characters.

　　1）啤酒多少钱一杯？/一杯啤酒多少钱？/多少钱一杯啤酒？/啤酒一杯多少钱？
　　2）一张光盘十五块太贵了，便宜点儿，行吗？/光盘十五块一张太贵了，能不能便宜点儿？
　　3）我要买一张中国音乐光盘。我很喜欢中国音乐。
　　4）这本书多少钱？
　　5）大的五块钱一瓶，小的三块一瓶。
　　6）一瓶啤酒(和)两瓶可乐一共多少钱？

Lesson 13
听力练习　Listening Practice

1. Listen to the reconding and fill in the correct times on the clocks.

　　　　1) 7:15 am　2) 8:55 am　3) 2:00 pm　4) 7:00 pm

2. Listen to the short dialogues and circle the correct answer in each group, accordingly.

　　1) a　　　　2) c　　　　3) b　　　　4) c　　　　5) b　　　　6) c　　　　7) c　　　　8) a

语法练习　Grammar Practice

1. Multiple choice.

　　1) a　　　　2) c　　　　3) a　　　　4) b　　　　5) c　　　　6) a

2. Put the words in each group in the correct order to create sentences.

　　1）北京烤鸭六十八块五一盘。
　　2）商店天天早上八点半开门。
　　3）你几点坐车回家？
　　4）我家附近有一个小水果店。
　　5）那个交换学生不认识汉字。
　　6）图书馆星期六晚上九点关门。

认字识词　Words with Known Characters

Figure out the English meanings of each of the words below and write them in the spaces provided.

课本	textbook	课外	after class
门口	entrance	大门	gate
换钱	change money	校车	school bus
近期	recently	学期	term/semester
新年	new year	新生	new student
开关	switch	交朋友	make friends

翻译练习　Translation

Say the following sentences in Chinese first, and then write them out in characters.

1) 现在几点（了）？　十二点差一刻。/十一点四十五。
2) 大英图书馆星期天几点开门?
3) 苹果多少钱一斤?
4) 苹果两块八一斤。
5) 我们图书馆早上七点半开门，晚上十点关门。
6. 他工作很忙，差不多天天晚上八点回家。

Lesson 14

听力练习　Listening Practice

Listen to the short dialogues and circle the correct answer in each group, accordingly.

1) c　　　2) a　　　3) b　　　4) c　　　5) c　　　6) b　　　7) a　　　8) c

语法练习　Grammar Practice

1. Multiple choice.

1) b　　　2) c　　　3) c　　　4) a　　　5) b　　　6) c

2. Fill in the blank with the words given. The first one has been done as an example.

2) b　　　3) c　　　4) e　　　5) d　　　6) f

认字识词　Words with Known Characters

Figure out the English meanings of each of the words below and write them in the spaces provided.

红茶	black tea	绿茶	green tea
药水	liquid medicine	药片	tablet
药酒	medicinal liquor	开发	develop
休学	suspension of schooling	休想	Don't think about it.
公路	highway	铁路	railway
路灯	streetlight	问路	ask way

翻译练习　Translation

Say the following sentences in Chinese first, and then write them out in characters.

1) 你有点感冒。你要多休息，多喝水。
2) 从我家到学校走路只要五分钟。
3) 请问去火车站怎么走?
4) 一直向前走，到红绿灯向右拐。
5) 你想吃中药还是吃西药?
6) 从医院走路去药店要几分钟?

Lesson 15

听力练习　Listening Practice

Listen to the short dialogues and circle the correct answer in each group, accordingly.

1) b　　2) a　　3) b　　4) c　　5) a　　6) c　　7) c　　8) a

语法练习　Grammar Practice

1. Multiple choice.

1) a　　2) c　　3) c　　4) b　　5) b　　6) a

2. Fill in the blanks with the words given.

1) a　　2) c　　3) f　　4) d　　5) b　　6) e

认字识词　Words with Known Characters

Figure out the English meanings of each of the words below and write them in the spaces provided.

生病	fall ill	病人	patient
南极	South Pole	北极	North Pole
民间	folk, unofficial	国民	citizen, national
金币	gold (coin)	机票	flight ticket
门票	entrance ticket	车票	travel ticket (for a land vehicle)
经常	often	非常	unusual, very

翻译练习　Translation

Say the following sentences in Chinese first, and then write them out in characters.

1) 现在十二月了，天气冷了。
2) 我以前踢足球,可是我现在打太极拳了。
3) 100英镑可以换多少美元?
4) 伦敦的中国饭既便宜，也好吃。
5) 他比以前瘦了。
6) 我没有现金，我只有旅行支票。

Lesson 16

听力练习　Listening Practice

Listen to the short dialogues and circle the correct answer in each group, accordingly. Each dialogue has two questions.

1) c　　2) b　　3) a　　4) a　　5) b　　6) a　　7) c　　8) c

语法练习　Grammar Practice

1. Multiple choice.

1) b　　2) a　　3) b　　4) c　　5) a　　6) a

2. Complete the following dialogues with the words provided.

1) 我是坐地铁来的。
2) 我是在伦敦大学学的。
3) 我是去年九月开始学的。
4) 我学了一年半了。
5) 我是和我女朋友一起去的。
6) 我们是在大英图书馆认识的。

认字识词　Words with Known Characters

Figure out the English meanings of each of the words below and write them in the spaces provided.

爱国	patriotic	爱人	spouse
交通	transportation	远东	Far East
等车	wait for a bus/train	赛车	car race
近视	short-sighted	远视	far sighted
出生	be born	出口	export/exit
商场	shopping centre	总共	altogether

翻译练习　Translation

Say the following sentences in Chinese first, and then write them out in characters.

1) 你们今天早上是怎么来的？我们是坐公共汽车来的。
2) 他以前常常坐出租车，现在很少坐了。
3) 学校离商店不远。走路只要十分钟。
4) 看来他们是昨晚到的。
5) 我们是在中国认识的。
6) 我现在不常去看足球赛了,因为我太太不喜欢看。

Lesson 17

听力练习　Listening Practice

Listen to the short dialogues and circle the correct answer in each group, accordingly. Each dialogue has two or three questions.

1) b　　　2) c　　　3) a　　　4) a　　　5) b　　　6) c　　　7) a　　　8) a

语法练习　Grammar Practice

1. Multiple choice.

1) a　　　2) b　　　3) b　　　4) a　　　5) b　　　6) c

2. Use the words provided in brackets to re-write the following sentences.

1) 图书馆星期六十点半就开门了。
2) 我们下个星期就开始上课了。
3) 足球赛五点半才开始。
4) 我今天早上七点才吃早饭。
5) 他跳舞跳得好极了。
6) 王先生汉语说得流利极了。

认字识词　Words with Known Characters

Figure out the English meanings of each of the words below and write them in the spaces provided.

流行	in vogue, popular	歌星	pop star
说话	talk; speak	电话	telephone
海边	seaside	海菜	seaweed
公海	public sea	大海	large sea; ocean
跳高	high jump	跳远	long jump
舞厅	ball room	舞会	ball

翻译练习　Translation

Say the following sentences in Chinese first, and then write them out in characters.
1) 你中文说得真好，比我说得好多了。
2) 他(开)车开得怎么样？他开得不错。
3) 你学了多长时间的中文了？一年半了。
4) 他们早上六点半就来了，怪不得他们很累。
5) 你怎么(这么晚)才来？他们半小时以前就到了。
6) 我们都知道学习汉语不容易。

Lesson 18

听力练习　Listening Practice

Listen to the short dialogues, and circle the correct answer in each group, accordingly. Each dialogue has two or three questions.

　　　1) b　　　2) b　　　3) a　　　4) c　　　5) b　　　6) c　　　7) b　　　8) a

语法练习　Grammar Practice

1. Multiple choice.
　　　1) c　　　2) a　　　3) c　　　4) b　　　5) a　　　6) c

2. Change the following sentences into their negative forms.
1) 他普通话说得不好。
2) 他没(有)看两遍。
3) 昨天晚上九点我没/不在看电视。
4) 星期天我没写两个小时的汉字。
5) 今天早上我不是坐公共汽车来的。
6) 张先生现在不在开会。

认字识词　Words with Known Characters

Figure out the English meanings of each of the words below and write them in the spaces provided.

爱情	love	情人	lover
考题	exam topic/question	电灯	electric light
用功	hard working	试用	tryout
接见	meet	接近	get close, access
零钱	change	借钱	borrow money
女子	woman	睡美人	Sleeping Beauty

翻译练习　Translation

Say the following sentences in Chinese first, and then write them out in characters.
1) 你在干什么呢？我在找我的书。
2) 昨天我去看他的时候，他（正）在给他的医生打电话。
3) 外面正在下雨。我以为你今天不来了。
4) 我最近在准备考试。今天下午得去买本新字典。
5) 我妈妈喜欢一边唱歌，一边做饭。
6) 昨天上午十点我不在开会,我在上汉语课。

Lesson 19

听力练习　Listening Practice

Listen to the recording, and circle the correct answer in each group, accordingly. Each dialogue or statement has two or three questions.

1) b　　　2) a　　　3) c　　　4) a　　　5) b　　　6) c　　　7) a　　　8) b

语法练习　Grammar Practice

1. Choose the correct position for 的 in the following sentences.

1) C　　　2) B　　　3) B　　　4) B　　　5) A　　　6) B

2. Fill in the blanks of each of the following sentences using 一边 ... 一边 ... or 又 ... 又....

1) 她<u>又</u>高<u>又</u>瘦。
2) 我妈妈做的菜<u>又</u>好吃，<u>又</u>好看。
3) 张先生总是<u>一边</u>喝酒，<u>一边</u>看足球赛。
4) 我<u>又</u>累<u>又</u>渴。
5) 我喜欢<u>一边</u>看书，<u>一边</u>听音乐。
6) 我们<u>一边</u>走，<u>一边</u>唱吧。

3. Multiple choice.

1) a　　　2) c　　　3) a　　　4) c　　　5) a　　　6) b

认字识词　Words with Known Characters

Figure out the English meanings of each of the words below and write them in the spaces provided.

前进	march on	进来	come in
礼品	gift	产地	place of production
人造	man-made	手工	handwork
车牌	car plate	王牌	ace card
生手	new hand	孩子	child, children
趣事	interesting story	提高	raise

翻译练习　Translation

Say the following sentences in Chinese first, and then write them out in characters.

1) 他爸爸昨天做的烤鸭真好吃。
2) 你认识在那儿和我们老师说话的女孩吗？
3) 这是我男朋友去年送给我的生日礼物。
4) 这是新产品，又好看又便宜。
5) 这个手机非常漂亮，可是不是最新产品，有点过时了。
6) 在火车站外边卖水果的那个人是我朋友的爸爸。

Lesson 20

听力练习　Listening Practice

Listen to the recording, and circle the correct answer in each group, accordingly. Each dialogue or statement has two or three questions.

1) a　　　2) b　　　3) c　　　4) b　　　5) c　　　6) a　　　7) a　　　8) b

语法练习　Grammar Practice

1. Please fill in the blanks with 了 or 过.

1) 了　　2) 过　　3) 了　　4) 了　　5) 过,了　　6) 过,了　　7) 过　　8) 了

2. Arrange the words in the correct order to make sentences.
1) 我学了两年的法语了。
2) 李老师打算去了(上海/海南)去(海南/上海)。
3) 你知道他去没去过中国？
4) 他们说黄山最美。
5) 我们马上就要到北京了。
6) 他/我从来没看过我/他写的小说。

认字识词　Words with Known Characters

Figure out the English meanings of each of the words below and write them in the spaces provided.

听写	dictation	北极熊	polar bear
放学	after school	骑马	horse ride
赛马	horse race	马路	road
山路	mountain road	山水	mountain and water
亚洲	Asia	非洲	Africa
北美洲	North America	南美洲	South America

翻译练习　Translation

Say the following sentences in Chinese first, and then write them out in characters.
1) 火车就要开了，请马上上车。
2) 学校一放假，黄小姐就去中国。
3) 我妹妹说熊猫是最可爱的动物。
4) 我爸爸去过上海，可是他从来没有去过北京。
5) 我以前没喝过中国啤酒，可是今天我要喝一杯。
6) 他们马上就要去欧洲大陆度假了。

附录五　Appendix 5

汉英词汇表　　Chinese-English Vocabulary List

啊	a	*pt*	ah (exclamation of surprise, etc.)	17
爱	ài	*v*	love; like very much	16
百	bǎi	*num*	hundred	12
半	bàn	*n*	half	13
帮	bāng	*v*	help	18
镑	bàng	*n*	pound sterling	15
北边	běibian	*n/l.w*	north	11
备	bèi	*v*	prepare	18
本	běn	*m.w*	for books	12
笔	bǐ	*n*	pen, pencil	18
比赛	bǐsài	*n/v*	match; have a match	16
笔试	bǐshì	*n*	written exam	18
币	bì	*n*	currency	15
边	biān	*n*	side	11
遍	biàn	*m.w*	times (for verbs)	17
表	biǎo	*v*	show	17
表演	biǎoyǎn	*v/n*	perform; performance	17
比利时	Bǐlìshí	*p.n*	Belgium	20
病	bìng	*n*	disease	15
不错	búcuò	*adj*	correct; not bad, pretty good	17
不过	búguò	*conj*	however	16
不舒服	bù shūfu	*adj*	unwell, uncomfortable	14
不怎么样	bù zěnmeyàng	*i.e*	not up to much	17
才	cái	*adv*	not...until, only	17
餐	cān	*n*	food, meal	13
餐厅	cāntīng	*n*	canteen	13
差	chà	*v*	lack, be short of	13
差不多	chàbuduō	*adj/adv*	similar; almost, nearly	13
产	chǎn	*v*	produce	19
产品	chǎnpǐn	*n*	product	19
长	cháng	*adj*	long	16

长城	Chángchéng	*n*	Great Wall	20
长江	Chángjiāng	*n*	Yangtze River	20
场	chǎng	*m.w/n*	for a match; field	16
唱	chàng	*v*	sing	17
唱歌	chànggē	*v-o*	sing	17
成	chéng	*v*	succeed; become	17
成功	chénggōng	*v/n*	succeed; success	17
城	chéng	*n*	city; wall	20
出	chū	*v*	go out	16
出租	chūzū	*v*	rent	16
出租车	chūzūchē	*n*	taxi	16
川	chuān	*p.n/n*	Sichuan (abbr.); flat river or land	20
次	cì	*m.w*	times (for verbs)	14
从	cóng	*prep*	from	14
从来	cónglái	*adv*	always, all along	17
从来不	cónglái bù	*adv*	never	17
错	cuò	*adj*	wrong, incorrect	17
打电话	dǎ diànhuà	*v-o*	make a phone call	18
打工	dǎgōng	*v*	work as a casual worker	18
大陆	dàlù	*n*	continent	20
大使	dàshǐ	*n*	ambassador	11
大使馆	dàshǐguǎn	*n*	embassy	11
大熊猫	dàxióngmāo	*n*	panda	20
大英图书馆	Dàyīng Túshūguǎn	*p.n*	the British Library	11
当	dāng	*prep*	just as, on the spot	19
当然	dāngrán	*adv*	of course; certainly	20
当时	dāngshí	*n*	at that time	19
到	dào	*prep/v*	to; arrive	14
道	dào	*n/v*	way; say	17
打算	dǎsuàn	*v/n*	plan	20
打针	dǎzhēn	*v-o*	inject	14
得	de	*pt*	verb complement marker	17
得	děi	*m.v*	have to	15
德	dé	*p.n/n*	Germany (abbr.); virtue	20
德国	Déguó	*p.n*	Germany	20

灯	dēng	*n*	light	14
等	děng	*v*	wait	16
第*	dì		prefix for ordinal numbers	14
点	diǎn	*n*	o'clock	13
典	diǎn	*n*	decree; classics	18
电话	diànhuà	*n*	telephone	18
电脑	diànnǎo	*n*	computer	19
电子	diànzǐ	*n*	electronics	18
跌	diē	*v*	fall down	15
定	dìng	*adv*	definitely	16
东北边	dōngběibian	*n/l.w*	northeast	11
东西	dōngxi	*n*	thing; object	19
懂	dǒng	*v*	understand	17
动	dòng	*v*	move	20
动物	dòngwù	*n*	animal	20
动物园	dòngwùyuán	*n*	zoo	20
度	dù	*v/n*	pass, spend	20
度假	dùjià	*v-o*	go on vacation	20
对了	duì le	*i.e*	oh, yes	18
对面	duìmiàn	*l.w*	opposite side	11
多长	duō cháng	*q.w*	how long	16
多少	duōshao	*q.w*	how much; how many	12
发	fā	*v*	become; develop	14
发烧	fāshāo	*v*	have a fever	14
方	fāng	*n*	prescription	14
放	fàng	*v*	release; put	20
放假	fàngjià	*v-o*	be on vacation	20
饭馆儿	fànguǎnr	*n*	restaurant	18
饭后	fàn hòu	*n*	after a meal	14
非*	fēi	*n*	Africa (abbr.)	11
飞	fēi	*v*	fly	20
飞机	fēijī	*n*	plane	20
飞机票	fēijīpiào	*n*	plane ticket	20
分	fēn	*m.w*	1/10 of a jiǎo; minute	12
分钟	fēnzhōng	*n*	minute	14

服	fú	v	be accustomed to	14
夫	fū	n	man; husband	17
附	fù	v	attach, add	13
附近	fùjìn	n	nearby	13
感	gǎn	v	be affected; feel	14
感冒	gǎnmào	v/n	catch cold; cold	14
感兴趣	gǎn xìngqu	v-o	be interested in	19
干	gàn	v	do (colloquial)	18
刚	gāng	adv	just (time)	16
高兴	gāoxìng	adj	pleased	19
歌	gē	n	song	17
各	gè	pron	each	19
给	gěi	v	give	18
跟	gēn	prep/v/conj	with; from; follow; and	17
公	gōng		prefix for metric units	15
公斤	gōngjīn	m.w	kilogram	15
公园	gōngyuán	n	park	11
功	gōng	n	achievement	17
功夫	gōngfu	n	kong fu (Chinese martial art)	17
拐	guǎi	v	turn	14
怪	guài	adj	strange; blame	17
怪不得	guàibudé	adv	no wonder	17
关	guān	v	close, turn off	13
关门	guān mén	v-o	close	13
关系	guānxi	n	relation	16
光	guāng	n	light, bright	12
光盘	guāngpán	n	CD	12
国家	guójiā	n	country, nation state	20
国王十字	Guōwáng Shízì	n	King's Cross (place name)	11
果	guǒ	n	fruit	13
过	guò	v	pass through, spend	16
过时	guòshí	adj	dated, out of date	19
还	hái	adv	even; in addition	17
孩	hái	n	child	19
海南	Hǎinán	p.n	Hainan (province)	20

行	háng	*n*	shop; firm	11
河	hé	*n*	river	20
很少	hěn shǎo	*adv*	seldom	15
红绿灯	hónglǜdēng	*n*	traffic lights	14
后	hòu	*n*	behind	11
后面	hòumiàn	*n/l.w*	behind	11
候*	hòu	*n*	time	13
花	huā	*v/n*	spend, take (time, money); flower	16
话	huà	*n*	speech	17
坏	huài	*adj*	out of order; bad; rotten	16
换	huàn	*v*	change	13
黄	huáng	*adj/p.n*	yellow; a surname	20
黄河	Huánghé	*n*	Yellow River	20
黄山	Huáng Shān	*n*	Huangshan (mountain)	20
回头见	huítóu jiàn	*i.e*	see you later	17
火车站	huǒchēzhàn	*n*	train station	11
机	jī	*n*	machine	19
极	jí	*n*	pole	15
极	jí	*adv*	extremely	17
既…也…	jì…yě…	*conj*	as well as	15
假	jià	*n*	holiday, leave	20
间	jiān	*n*	between	11
江	jiāng	*n*	large river	20
交	jiāo	*v*	cross; make	13
交换	jiāohuàn	*v*	exchange	13
角	jiǎo	*m.w*	1/10 a yuán	12
觉	jiào	*n*	nap, sleep	18
接	jiē	*v*	meet; connect	18
借	jiè	*v*	borrow; lend	18
斤	jīn	*m.w*	Chinese weight unit equal to ½ kilogram	13
金	jīn	*n*	gold	15
近	jìn	*adj*	near, close	13
进	jìn	*v*	come in, move forward	19
进口	jìnkǒu	*n*	import	19
经	jīng	*prep/adv*	through	15

久	jiǔ	*adj/adv*	long time	16
开	kāi	*v*	boil	14
开会	kāihuì	*v-o*	hold/attend a meeting	17
开门	kāi mén	*v-o*	open	13
开始	kāishǐ	*v*	start, begin	13
开水	kāishuǐ	*n*	boiled/boiling water	14
开晚会	kāi wǎnhuì	*v-o*	have an evening party	17
看病	kàn bìng	*v-o*	see a doctor	15
看来	kànlái	*v*	seem	16
考	kǎo	*v*	test; inspect	18
考试	kǎoshì	*v*	take an exam	18
刻	kè	*n*	quarter (hour)	13
课	kè	*n*	lesson	13
可爱	kěài	*adj*	lovely	20
可乐	kělè	*n*	cola	12
可以	kěyǐ	*m.v*	may; can	14
口试	kǒushì	*v/n*	oral exam	18
块	kuài	*m.w*	a colloquial term for yuán	12
矿	kuàng	*n*	mine	12
矿泉水	kuàngquánshuǐ	*n*	mineral water	12
离	lí	*v*	leave; separate	16
离开	líkāi	*v*	depart, leave	16
里	lǐ	*n*	inside	11
里面	lǐmiàn	*l.w*	inside	11
礼	lǐ	*n*	ritual; courteous	19
礼物	lǐwù	*n*	gift, present	19
利	lì	*adj/n*	sharp; benefit	17
练	liàn	*v*	practise	18
练习	liànxí	*v/n*	exercise	18
零	líng	*num*	zero	15
流	liú	*v*	flow	17
流利	liúlì	*adj*	fluent	17
陆	lù	*n*	land; land mass	20
旅	lǚ	*n/v*	travel	15
旅行	lǚxíng	*n*	travel	15

绿	lǜ	*n*	green	14
马	mǎ	*n*	horse	20
马上	mǎshàng	*adv*	right away	20
买	mǎi	*v*	buy	12
卖	mài	*v*	sell	12
毛	máo	*m.w*	a colloquial term for jiǎo	12
冒	mào	*v*	risk	14
没关系	méi guānxi	*i.e*	it doesn't matter	16
美	měi	*p.n/adj*	USA (abbr.); beautiful	15
美国	Měiguó	*p.n*	USA	19
美元	měiyuán	*n*	US dollar	15
门	mén	*n*	door	13
面	miàn	*n*	side, face	11
民	mín	*n*	folk, people	15
明信片	míngxìnpiàn	*n*	postcard	12
那	nà	*conj*	in that case; then	12
那么	nàme	*adv*	so	15
那儿	nàr	*pron/l.w*	there	19
南	nán	*n*	south	11
南面	nánmiàn	*n/l.w*	south	11
脑	nǎo	*n*	brain	19
能	néng	*m.v*	can, be able to	12
女孩儿	nǚháir	*n*	girl	19
欧	Ōu	*n*	Europe (abbr.)	15
欧元	ōuyuán	*n*	euro	15
欧洲	Ōuzhōu	*n*	Europe	20
牌	pái	*n*	card, plaque	19
牌子	páizi	*n*	brand (product)	19
旁	páng	*n*	side	11
旁边	pángbiān	*n/l.w*	side	11
便*	pián	*adj*	cheap	12
便宜	piányi	*adj*	cheap	12
片	piàn	*n*	card	12
片	piàn	*m.w*	for tablets	14
票	piào	*n*	ticket	15

品	pǐn	*n*	item, goods	19
苹*	píng	*n*	apple	13
苹果	píngguǒ	*n*	apple	13
普	pǔ	*adj*	ordinary	17
普通	pǔtōng	*adj*	ordinary, common	17
普通话	pǔtōnghuà	*n*	Mandarin; common speech	17
前	qián	*n*	front	11
钱	qián	*n*	money	12
前头	qiántou	*n/l.w*	front	11
千	qiān	*num*	thousand	15
请	qǐng	*v*	please; invite	11
情	qíng	*n*	affection, feeling	18
情书	qíngshū	*n*	love letter	18
趣	qù	*n*	interest	19
泉	quán	*n*	spring	12
拳	quán	*n*	fist	15
然	rán	*pron*	thus, so	14
然后	ránhòu	*conj*	then	14
让	ràng	*v*	make, let; ask; allow	16
人民	rénmín	*n*	people	15
人民币	rénmínbì	*n*	RMB (Chinese currency)	15
认真	rènzhēn	*adj/adv*	conscientious; earnest	19
日本	Rìběn	*p.n*	Japan	13
容易	róngyì	*adj*	easy	17
赛	sài	*n*	match, competition	16
山	shān	*n*	mountain	20
上半场	shàng bànchǎng	*n*	the first half (of a match)	16
上课	shàngkè	*v*	have classes	13
上午	shàngwǔ	*n/t.w*	morning	13
上涨	shàngzhǎng	*v*	rise	15
生产	shēngchǎn	*v*	produce, make	19
十字路口	shízì lùkǒu	*n*	crossroad	14
时	shí	*n*	time; hour	13
时候	shíhou	*n*	time; when	13
时间	shíjiān	*n*	time	16

使	shǐ	*n*	messenger	11
始	shǐ	*v*	begin	13
事	shì	*n*	matter; business	18
试	shì	*v*	test; try	18
收	shōu	*v*	accept; receive	15
手	shǒu	*n*	hand	19
手机	shǒujī	*n*	mobile phone	19
手提	shǒutí	*adj*	portable	19
书店	shūdiàn	*n*	bookstore	11
舒*	shū	*adj*	easy	14
舒服	shūfu	*adj*	comfortable	14
水	shuǐ	*n*	water	12
水果	shuǐguǒ	*n*	fruit	13
水果店	shuǐguǒdiàn	*n*	fruit shop	13
睡	shuì	*v*	sleep	18
睡觉	shuìjiào	*v/n*	sleep	18
四川	Sìchuān	*n*	Sichuan (province)	20
送	sòng	*v*	give sth. as a present; see someone off	12
算	suàn	*v*	calculate	20
所	suǒ	*adv*	actually; that which	16
所以	suǒyǐ	*conj*	so, therefore	16
台	tái	*m.w*	for machines	19
太极拳	tàijíquán	*n*	tai chi	15
疼	téng	*v*	hurt, pain	14
题	tí	*n*	topic; title	18
提	tí	*v*	pick up; lift	19
跳	tiào	*v*	jump	17
跳舞	tiàowǔ	*v-o/n*	dance	17
厅	tīng	*n*	hall	13
听	tīng	*v*	listen, hear	19
听课	tīngkè	*v*	listen to/attend a lecture	19
听说	tīngshuō	*v*	it is said; people say	20
通	tōng	*adj*	common, general	16
通常	tōngcháng	*adv*	usually	16
头	tóu	*n*	end; head	11

外面	wàimiàn	*l.w*	outside	11
玩儿	wánr	*v*	play; have fun	20
忘	wàng	*v*	forget	19
问	wèn	*v*	ask (a question)	11
问题	wèntí	*n*	question, problem	18
午	wǔ	*n*	noon	13
舞	wǔ	*n*	dance	17
物	wù	*n*	thing, object	19
西	xī	*n*	west	11
西班牙	Xībānyá	*p.n*	Spain	20
西方	xīfāng	*n*	the West	12
西南面	xīnánmiàn	*n/l.w*	southwest	11
息	xī	*v*	rest	14
习	xí	*v*	practice	18
系	xì	*n*	tie; department	16
下跌	xiàdiē	*v*	fall	15
下午	xiàwǔ	*t.w*	afternoon	13
现	xiàn	*n*	now	13
现金	xiànjīn	*n*	cash	15
现在	xiànzài	*t.w*	now	13
向	xiàng	*prep*	towards	14
小时	xiǎoshí	*n*	hour	13
小说	xiǎoshuō	*n*	novel	12
校	xiào	*n*	school, college	13
些	xiē	*n*	some	20
新	xīn	*adj*	new	13
信	xìn	*n*	letter	12
信	xìn	*v*	believe	17
行	xíng	*adj*	all right, OK; competent	12
兴	xìng	*adj*	pleased	19
兴趣	xìngqu	*n*	interest	19
熊	xióng	*n*	bear	20
休	xiū	*v*	cease	14
休息	xiūxi	*v*	rest, break	14
需	xū	*v*	need	16

需要	xūyào	v	need	16
学校	xuéxiào	n	school, college	13
牙	yá	n	tooth	20
亚*	yà	n	Asia (abbr.)	11
亚非学院	Yàfēi Xuéyuàn	p.n	SOAS	11
演	yǎn	v	perform	17
药	yào	n	medicine, drug	14
药店	yàodiàn	n	pharmacy	14
药方	yàofāng	n	prescription	14
要	yào	v/m.v	need, want; should	14
一半	yíbàn	n	half	16
一共	yígòng	adv	altogether	12
一定	yídìng	adv	surely, definitely	16
一下	yíxià	adv	for a while, briefly; once	18
一直	yìzhí	adv	straight forward	14
一边儿…一边儿…	yìbiānr…yìbiānr…	conj	while … while … (linking two concurrent activities)	18
以	yǐ	v/ prep	take; according to	14
以后	yǐhòu	adv	after, later on, afterwards	16
以前	yǐqián	n	before, ago	15
以为	yǐwéi	v	assume (wrongly); think	18
已	yǐ	adv	already	15
已经	yǐjīng	adv	already	15
宜*	yí	adj	appropriate	12
意	yì	p.n/n	Italy (abbr.); intention; meaning	20
意大利	Yìdàlì	p.n	Italy	20
音	yīn	n	sound	12
音乐	yīnyuè	n	music	12
银	yín	n	silver	11
英镑	yīngbàng	n	pound sterling	15
银行	yínháng	n	bank	11
用	yòng	v	use; with	18
有时候	yǒushíhou	adv	sometimes	16
右	yòu	n	right	11
右面	yòumiàn	n/l.w	right side	11

又	yòu	*adv*	again, once more	19
又…又…	yòu…yòu…	*conj*	both ... and ...	19
园	yuán	*n*	garden	11
元	yuán	*m.w*	unit of Chinese currency (RMB)	12
远	yuǎn	*adj*	far	16
乐	yuè	*n*	music	12
云	yún	*n*	cloud	20
云南	Yúnnán	*n*	Yunnan (province)	20
在	zài	*v/prep*	be at/in/on; at/in/on	11
早饭	zǎofàn	*n*	breakfast	13
造	zào	*v*	create, make	19
站	zhàn	*n*	station	11
张	Zhāng	*n*	Zhang (a surname)	11
张	zhāng	*m.w*	for paper, postcards, CDs, etc.	12
涨	zhǎng	*v*	rise	15
找	zhǎo	*v*	give change; find, look for	12
这么	zhème	*adv*	so	13
针	zhēn	*n*	needle	14
真	zhēn	*adv/adj*	really; true	16
真的	zhēn de	*adv*	really	16
正	zhèng	*adv*	just then, at that point	18
支	zhī	*v*	pay	15
支票	zhīpiào	*n*	cheque	15
直	zhí	*adj*	straight	14
制	zhì	*v*	make	19
制造	zhìzào	*v*	make, manufacture	19
中间	zhōngjiān	*n/l.w*	in the middle of	11
钟	zhōng	*n*	clock	14
种	zhǒng	*m.w*	kind, type	19
洲	zhōu	*n*	continent	20
准	zhǔn	*v*	adjust	18
准备	zhǔnbèi	*v/n*	prepare; preparation	18
子*	zǐ		(noun suffix)	18
字典	zìdiǎn	*n*	dictionary	18
总	zǒng	*adj*	general, chief	16

附录五 Appendix 5

总是	zǒngshì	*adv*	always	16
租	zū	*v*	rent	16
最	zuì	*adv*	most	18
最近	zuìjìn	*adv*	recently	18
昨*	zuó	*n*	last (in 昨天 and 昨晚)	15
昨天	zuótiān	*n*	yesterday	15
左	zuǒ	*n*	left	11
左面	zuǒmiàn	*n/l.w*	left side	11
左右	zuǒyòu	*adv*	about, approximately	13

附录六　Appendix 6

英汉词汇表　English-Chinese Vocabulary List

1/10 of a jiǎo; minute	分	fēn	m.w	12
1/10 of a yuán	角	jiǎo	m.w	12
a colloquial term for jiǎo	毛	máo	m.w	12
a colloquial term for yuán	块	kuài	m.w	12
about, approximately	左右	zuǒyòu	adv	13
accept; receive	收	shōu	v	15
achievement	功	gōng	n	17
actually; that which	所	suǒ	adv	16
actually	所以	suǒ	adv	16
adjust	准	zhǔn	v	18
affection, feeling	情	qíng	n	18
Africa (abbr.)	非	fēi	n	11
after a meal	饭后	fànhòu	n	14
after, later on, afterwards	以后	yǐhòu	adv	16
afternoon	下午	xiàwǔ	t.w	13
again, once more	又	yòu	adv	19
ah(exclamation of surprise, etc.)	啊	a	pt	17
all right, OK; competent	行	xíng	adj	12
already	已	yǐ	adv	15
already	已经	yǐjīng	adv	15
altogether	一共	yígòng	adv	12
always	总是	zǒngshì	adv	16
always, all along	从来	cónglái	adv	17
ambassador	大使	dàshǐ	n	11
animal	动物	dòngwù	n	20
apple	苹*	píng	n	13
apple	苹果	píngguǒ	n	13
appropriate	宜*	yí	adj	12
as well as	既…也…	jì…yě…	conj	15
Asia (abbr.)	亚*	yà	n	11
ask (a question)	问	wèn	v	11

assume (wrongly); think	以为	yǐwéi	*v*	18
at that time	当时	dāngshí	*n*	19
attach, add	附	fù	*v*	13
bank	银行	yínháng	*n*	11
be accustomed to	服	fú	*v*	14
be affected; feel	感	gǎn	*v*	14
be at/in/on: at/in/on	在	zài	*v/prep*	11
be on vacation	放假	fàngjià	*v-o*	20
be interested in	感兴趣	gǎnxìngqu	*v-o*	19
bear	熊	xióng	*n*	20
become; develop	发	fā	*v*	14
before, ago	以前	yǐqián	*n*	15
begin	始	shǐ	*v*	13
behind	后	hòu	*n*	11
behind	后面	hòumiàn	*n/l.w*	11
Belgium	比利时	Bǐlìshí	*p.n*	20
believe	信	xìn	*v*	17
between	间	jiān	*n*	11
boil	开	kāi	*v*	14
boiled/boiling water	开水	kāishuǐ	*n*	14
bookstore	书店	shūdiàn	*n*	11
borrow; lend	借	jiè	*v*	18
both ... and ...	又…又…	yòu...yòu...	*conj*	19
brain	脑	nǎo	*n*	19
brand (product)	牌子	páizi	*n*	19
breakfast	早饭	zǎofàn	*n*	13
British Library	大英图书馆	Dàyīng Túshūguǎn	*p.n*	11
buy	买	mǎi	*v*	12
calculate	算	suàn	*v*	20
can, be able to	能	néng	*m.v*	12
canteen	餐厅	cāntīng	*n*	13
card	片	piàn	*n*	12
card, plaque	牌	pái	*n*	19
cash	现金	xiànjīn	*n*	15
catch cold; cold	感冒	gǎnmào	*v/n*	14

CD	光盘	guāngpán	*n*	12
cease	休	xiū	*v*	14
change	换	huàn	*v*	13
cheap	便*	pián	*adj*	12
cheap	便宜	piányi	*adj*	12
cheque	支票	zhīpiào	*n*	15
child	孩	hái	*n*	19
Chinese weight unit equal to ½ kilogram	斤	jīn	*m.w*	13
city; wall	城	chéng	*n*	20
clock	钟	zhōng	*n*	14
close	关门	guān mén	*v-o*	13
close, turn off	关	guān	*v*	13
cloud	云	yún	*n*	20
cola	可乐	kělè	*n*	12
come in, move forward	进	jìn	*v*	19
comfortable	舒服	shūfu	*adj*	14
common, general	通	tōng	*adj*	16
computer	电脑	diànnǎo	*n*	19
conscientious; earnest	认真	rènzhēn	*adj*	19
continent	大陆	dàlù	*n*	20
continent	洲	zhōu	*n*	20
correct; not bad, pretty good	不错	búcuò	*adj*	17
country, nation state	国家	guójiā	*n*	20
create, make	造	zào	*v*	19
cross; make	交	jiāo	*v*	13
crossroad	十字路口	shízì lùkǒu	*n*	14
currency	币	bì	*n*	15
dance	跳舞	tiàowǔ	*v-o/n*	17
dance	舞	wǔ	*n*	17
dated, out of date	过时	guòshí	*adj*	19
decree; classics	典	diǎn	*n*	18
definitely	定	dìng	*adv*	16
depart, leave	离开	líkāi	*v*	16
desease	病	bìng	*n*	15
dictionary	字典	zìdiǎn	*n*	18

do (colloquial)	干	gàn	v	18
door	门	mén	n	13
each	各	gè	pron	19
easy	舒	shū	adj	14
easy	容易	róngyì	adj	17
electronics	电子	diànzǐ	n	18
embassy	大使馆	dàshǐguǎn	n	11
end; head	头	tóu	n	11
euro	欧元	ōuyuán	n	15
Europe	欧洲	Ōuzhōu	n	20
Europe (abbr.)	欧	Ōu	n	15
even; in addition	还	hái	adv	17
exchange	交换	jiāohuàn	v	13
exercise	练习	liànxí	v/n	18
extremely	极	jí	adv	17
fall	下跌	xiàdiē	v	15
fall down	跌	diē	v	15
far	远	yuǎn	adj	16
fist	拳	quán	n	15
flow	流	liú	v	17
fluent	流利	liúlì	adj	17
fly	飞	fēi	v	20
folk, people	民	mín	n	15
food, meal	餐	cān	n	13
for a match; field	场	chǎng	m.w/n	16
for a while, briefly; once	一下	yíxià	adv	18
for books	本	běn	m.w	12
for machines	台	tái	m.w	19
for paper, postcards, CDs, etc.	张	zhāng	m.w	12
for tablets	片	piàn	m.w	14
forget	忘	wàng	v	19
from	从	cóng	prep	14
front	前	qián	n	11
front	前头	qiántou	n	11
fruit	果	guǒ	n	13

fruit	水果	shuǐguǒ	*n*	13
fruit shop	水果店	shuǐguǒdiàn	*n*	13
garden	园	yuán	*n*	11
general, chief	总	zǒng	*adj*	16
Germany	德国	Déguó	*p.n*	20
Germany (abbr.); virtue	德	dé	*p.n/n*	20
gift, present	礼物	lǐwù	*n*	19
girl	女孩儿	nǚháir	*n*	19
give	给	gěi	*v*	18
give sth. as a present; see someone off	送	sòng	*v*	12
give change; find, look for	找	zhǎo	*v*	12
go on vacation	度假	dùjià	*v-o*	20
go out	出	chū	*v*	16
gold	金	jīn	*n*	15
Great Wall	长城	Chángchéng	*p.n*	20
green	绿	lǜ	*n*	14
Hainan (province)	海南	Hǎinán	*p.n*	20
half	半，一半	bàn	*n*	13,16
hall	厅	tīng	*n*	13
hand	手	shǒu	*n*	19
have a fever	发烧	fāshāo	*v*	14
have an evening party	开晚会	kāi wǎnhuì	*v-o*	17
have classes	上课	shàngkè	*v-o*	13
have to	得	děi	*m.v*	15
help	帮	bāng	*v*	18
hold/attend a meeting	开会	kāi huì	*v-o*	17
holiday, leave	假	jià	*n*	20
horse	马	mǎ	*n*	20
hour	小时	xiǎoshí	*n*	13
how long	多长	duō cháng	*q.w*	16
how much; how many	多少	duōshao	*q.w*	12
however	不过	búguò	*conj*	16
Huangshan (mountain)	黄山	Huángshān	*p.n*	20
hundred	百	bǎi	*num*	12
hurt, pain	疼	téng	*v*	14

import	进口	jìnkǒu	*n*	19
in that case; then	那	nà	*conj*	12
in the middle of	中间	zhōngjiān	*n/l.w*	11
inject	打针	dǎzhēn	*v-o*	14
inside	里	lǐ	*n*	11
inside	里面	lǐmiàn	*n/l.w*	11
interest	趣	qù	*n*	19
interest	兴趣	xìngqu	*n*	19
it doesn't matter	没关系	méi guānxi	*i.e*	16
it is said; people say	听说	tīngshuō	*v*	20
Italy	意大利	Yìdàlì	*p.n*	20
Italy (sort form) intention; meaning	意	yì	*p.n/n*	20
item, goods	品	pǐn	*n*	19
Japan	日本	Rìběn	*p.n*	13
jump	跳	tiào	*v*	17
just (time)	刚	gāng	*adv*	16
just as, on the spot	当	dāng	*prep*	19
just then, at that point	正	zhèng	*adv*	18
kilogram	公斤	gōngjīn	*m.w*	15
kind, type	种	zhǒng	*m.w*	19
King's Cross (place name)	国王十字	Guōwáng Shízì	*n*	11
kong fu (Chinese martial art)	功夫	gōngfu	*n*	17
lack, be short of	差	chà	*v*	13
land; land mass	陆	lù	*n*	20
large river	江	jiāng	*n*	20
later	后来	hòulái	*adv*	16
leave; separate	离	lí	*v*	16
left	左	zuǒ	*n*	11
left side	左面	zuǒmiàn	*n/l.w*	11
lesson	课	kè	*n*	13
letter	信	xìn	*n*	12
light	灯	dēng	*n*	14
light, bright	光	guāng	*n*	12
listen to/attend a lecture	听课	tīngkè	*v*	19
listen, hear	听	tīng	*v*	19

long	长	cháng	*adj*	16
long time	久	jiǔ	*adj/adv*	16
love letter	情书	qíngshū	*n*	18
love; like very much	爱	ài	*v*	16
lovely	可爱	kěài	*adj*	20
machine	机	jī	*n*	19
make	制	zhì	*v*	19
make a phone call	打电话	dǎ diànhuà	*v-o*	18
make, let; ask; allow	让	ràng	*v*	16
make, manufacture	制造	zhìzào	*v*	19
man; husband	夫	fū	*n*	17
Mandarin; common speech	普通话	pǔtōnghuà	*n*	17
match; have a match	比赛	bǐsài	*n/v*	16
match, competition	赛	sài	*n*	16
matter; business	事	shì	*n*	18
may; can	可以	kěyǐ	*m.v*	14
medicine, drug	药	yào	*n*	14
meet; connect	接	jiē	*v*	18
messenger	使	shǐ	*n*	11
mine	矿	kuàng	*n*	12
mineral water	矿泉水	kuàngquánshuǐ	*n*	12
minute	分钟	fēnzhōng	*n*	14
mobile phone	手机	shǒujī	*n*	19
money	钱	qián	*n*	12
morning	上午	shàngwǔ	*t.w*	13
most	最	zuì	*adv*	18
mountain	山	shān	*n*	20
move	动	dòng	*v*	20
music	音乐	yīnyuè	*n*	12
music	乐	yuè	*n*	12
nap, sleep	觉	jiào	*n*	18
near, close	近	jìn	*adj*	13
nearby	附近	fùjìn	*n*	13
need	需	xū	*v*	16
need	需要	xūyào	*v*	16

need, want; should	要	yào	v/m.v	14
needle	针	zhēn	n	14
never	从来不	cónglái bù	adv	17
new	新	xīn	adj	13
no wonder	怪不得	guàibudé	adv	17
noon	午	wǔ	n	13
north	北边	běibian	n	11
northeast	东北边	dōngběibian	n/l.w	11
not up to much	不怎么样	bù zěnmeyàng	i.e	17
not ... until, only	才	cái	adv	17
noun suffix	子*	zǐ		18
novel	小说	xiǎoshuō	n	12
now	现	xiàn	n	13
now	现在	xiànzài	t.w	13
o'clock	点	diǎn	n	13
of course, certainly	当然	dāngrán	adv	20
oh, yes	对了	duìle	i.e	18
open	开门	kāi mén	v-o	13
opposite side	对面	duìmiàn	n/l.w	11
oral exam	口试	kǒushì	v/n	18
ordinary	普	pǔ	adj	17
ordinary, common	普通	pǔtōng	adj	17
out of order; bad; rotten	坏	huài	adj	16
outside	外面	wàimiàn	n/l.w	11
panda	大熊猫	dàxióngmāo	n	20
park	公园	gōngyuán	n	11
pass through, spend	过	guò	v	16
pass, spend	度	dù	v	20
pay	支	zhī	v	15
pen, pencil	笔	bǐ	n	18
people	人民	rénmín	n	15
perform	演	yǎn	v	17
perform; performance	表演	biǎoyǎn	v/n	17
pharmacy	药店	yàodiàn	n	14
pick up; lift	提	tí	v	19

plan	打算	dǎsuàn	v/n	20
plane	飞机	fēijī	n	20
plane ticket	飞机票	fēijīpiào	n	20
play, have fun	玩儿	wánr	v	20
please; invite	请	qǐng	v	11
pleased	高兴	gāoxìng	adj	19
pleased	兴	xìng	adj	19
pole	极	jí	n	15
portable	手提	shǒutí	adj	19
postcard	明信片	míngxìnpiàn	n	12
pound sterling	镑	bàng	n	15
pound sterling	英镑	yīngbàng	n	15
practise	习	xí	v	18
practise	练	liàn	v	18
prefix for metric units	公	gōng		15
prefix for ordinal numbers	第*	dì		14
prepare	备	bèi	v	18
prepare; preparation	准备	zhǔnbèi	v/n	18
prescription	方	fāng	n	14
prescription	药方	yàofāng	n	14
produce	产	chǎn	n	19
produce, make	生产	shēngchǎn	v	19
product	产品	chǎnpǐn	n	19
quarter (hour)	刻	kè	n	13
question, problem	问题	wèntí	n	18
really	真的	zhēn de	adv	16
really; true	真	zhēn	adv/adj	16
recently	最近	zuìjìn	adv	18
relation	关系	guānxi	n	16
release; put	放	fàng	v	20
rent	出租	chūzū	v	16
rent	租	zū	v	16
rest	息	xī	v	14
rest, break	休息	xiūxi	v	14
restaurant	饭馆儿	fànguǎnr	n	11

right	右	yòu	n	11
right away	马上	mǎshàng	adv	20
right side	右面	yòumiàn	l.w	11
rise	上涨	shàngzhǎng	v	15
rise	涨	zhǎng	v	15
risk	冒	mào	v	14
ritual, courteous	礼	lǐ	n	19
river	河	hé	n	20
RMB (Chinese currency)	人民币	rénmínbì	n	15
school, college	校	xiào	n	13
school, college	学校	xuéxiào	n	13
see a doctor	看病	kànbìng	n	15
see you later	回头见	huítóu jiàn	v-o	17
seem	看来	kànlái	v	16
seldom	很少	hěn shǎo	adv	15
sell	卖	mài	v	12
sharp; benefit	利	lì	adj/n	17
shop, firm	行	háng	n	11
show	表	biǎo	v	17
Sichuan (province)	四川	Sìchuān	p.n	20
Sichuan (abbr.) ; flat river or land	川	chuān	p.n/n	20
side	旁边	pángbiān	l.w	11
side	边	biān	n	11
side	旁	páng	n	11
side; face	面	miàn	n	11
silver	银	yín	n	11
similar; almost, nearly	差不多	chàbuduō	adv	13
sing	唱	chàng	v	17
sing	唱歌	chànggē	v-o	17
sleep	睡	shuì	v	18
sleep	睡觉	shuìjiào	v/n	18
so	那么	nàme	adv	15
so	这么	zhème	adv	13
so, therefore	所以	suǒyǐ	conj	16
SOAS	亚非学院	Yàfēi Xuéyuàn	p.n	11

some	些	xiē	*n*	20
sometimes	有时候	yǒu shíhou	*adv*	16
song	歌	gē	*n*	17
sound	音	yīn	*n*	12
south	南	nán	*n*	11
south	南面	nánmiàn	*n/l.w*	11
southwest	西南面	xīnánmiàn	*n/l.w*	11
Spain	西班牙	Xībānyá	*p.n*	20
speech	话	huà	*n*	17
spend, take; flower	花	huā	*v/n*	16
spring	泉	quán	*n*	12
start, begin	开始	kāishǐ	*v*	13
station	站	zhàn	*n*	11
straight	直	zhí	*adj*	14
straight forward	一直	yìzhí	*adv*	14
strange; blame	怪	guài	*adj/v*	17
succeed; become	成	chéng	*v*	17
succeed; success	成功	chénggōng	*v/n*	17
surely; definitely	一定	yídìng	*adv*	16
tai chi	太极拳	tàijíquán	*n*	15
take an exam	考试	kǎoshì	*v*	18
taxi	出租车	chūzūchē	*n*	16
telephone	电话	diànhuà	*n*	18
test; inspect	考	kǎo	*v*	18
test; try	试	shì	*v*	18
the first half (of a match)	上半场	shàng bànchǎng	*n*	16
there	那儿	nàr	*pron/l.w*	19
then	然后	ránhòu	*conj*	14
thing, object	物	wù	*n*	19
thing, object	东西	dōngxi	*n*	19
thousand	千	qiān	*num*	15
through	经	jīng	*prep/adv*	15
thus, so	然	rán	*pron*	14
ticket	票	piào	*n*	15
tie; department	系	xì	*n*	16

time	候*	hòu	*n*	13
time	时间	shíjiān	*n*	16
time; hour	时	shí	*n*	13
time; when	时候	shíhou	*n*	13
times (for verb)	遍	biàn	*m.w*	17
times (for verb)	次	cì	*m.w*	14
to; arrive	到	dào	*prep/v*	14
tooth	牙	yá	*n*	20
topic; title	题	tí	*n*	18
towards	向	xiàng	*prep*	14
traffic lights	红绿灯	hónglùdēng	*n*	14
train station	火车站	huǒchēzhàn	*n*	11
travel	旅	lǚ	*n/v*	15
travel	旅行	lǚxíng	*n*	15
turn	拐	guǎi	*v*	14
understand	懂	dǒng	*v*	17
unit of Chinese currency RMB	元	yuán	*m.w*	12
unwell, uncomfortable	不舒服	bù shūfu	*adj*	14
US dollar	美元	měiyuán	*n*	15
USA	美国	Měiguó	*p.n*	19
USA (abbr.); beautiful	美	měi	*p.n/adj*	15
use; with	用	yòng	*v/prep*	18
usually	通常	tōngcháng	*adv*	16
verb complement marker	得	de	*pt*	17
wait	等	děng	*v*	16
water	水	shuǐ	*n*	12
way; say	道	dào	*n/v*	17
west	西	xī	*n*	11
West	西方	xīfāng	*n*	12
while...while...(linking two concurrent activities)	以	yǐ	*prep*	14
with, according to	一边儿…一边儿	yìbiānr...yìbiānr...	*conj*	18
with, from; follow; and	跟	gēn	*prep/v/conj*	17
work as a casual worker	打工	dǎgōng	*v*	18
written exam	笔试	bǐshì	*n*	18
wrong, incorrect	错	cuò	*adj*	17

Yangtze River	长江	Chángjiāng	*p.n*	20
Yellow River	黄河	Huánghé	*p.n*	20
yellow; a surname	黄	huáng	*adj/n*	20
yesterday	昨*	zuó	*n*	15
yesterday	昨天	zuótiān	*n*	15
Yunnan (province)	云南	Yúnnán	*p.n*	20
zero	零	líng	*num*	16
Zhang (a surname)	张	Zhāng	*n*	11
zoo	动物园	dòngwùyuán	*n*	20

附录七   Appendix 7

拼音文本 Pinyin Text for the Dialogues and Readings

Warming Up Lesson

Dialogue one

Wáng Jīng:	Xiǎo Lǐ, nǐ hǎo! Zhè shì wǒ de Zhōngguó péngyou Gāo Míng. Tā shì Dōngfāng Xuéyuàn de xuésheng.
Lǐ Dōng:	Nǐ hǎo! Wǒ shì Lúndūn Dàxué de xuésheng, Zhōngwén míngzi jiào Lǐ Dōng.
Gāo Míng:	Nǐ hǎo!
Lǐ Dōng:	Gāo Míng, nǐ shì Zhōngguó shénme dìfang rén?
Gāo Míng:	Jiào wǒ Xiǎo Gāo ba. Wǒ shì Běijīngrén.
Lǐ Dōng:	Hǎo. Wǒ yǒu gè péngyou Xiè Hóng yě shì Běijīngrén, yě shì Dōngfāng Xuéyuàn de xuésheng.
Gāo Míng:	Shì ma? Wǒ bú rènshi tā. Tā xué shénme zhuānyè?
Lǐ Dōng:	Tā xué shāngyè.
Wáng Jīng:	Xiǎo Lǐ, wǒmen jīntiān yǒu gè wǎnhuì, nǐ lái ma?
Lǐ Dōng:	Wǒ hěn xiǎng qù, kěshì wǒ jīntiān hěn máng.
Wáng Jīng:	Nǐ tiāntiān dōu hěn máng! Jīntiān shì Xiǎo Gāo de shēngri.
Lǐ Dōng:	Shì ma? Xiǎo Gāo, shēngri kuàilè!
Gāo Míng:	Xièxie.
Wáng Jīng:	Nǐmen è bu è? Wǒmen yìqǐ qù chī fàn, hǎo ma?
Lǐ Dōng:	Chī shénme? Chī sānmíngzhì?
Wáng Jīng:	Jīntiān shì Xiǎo Gāo de shēngri, wǒmen qù chī Zhōngguófàn ba.
Lǐ Dōng, Gāo Míng:	Hǎo. Wǒmen zǒu.

Dialogue Two

Lǐ Dōng:	Xiǎo Gāo, nǐ xǐhuan dǎ wǎngqiú ma?
Gāo Míng:	Xǐhuan.
Lǐ Dōng:	Wǒmen xīngqīliù yìqǐ qù dǎ wǎngqiú, hǎo bu hǎo?
Gāo Míng:	Xīngqīliù wǒ hěn máng. Xīngqītiān zěnmeyàng?
Lǐ Dōng:	Xīngqītiān wǒ xiǎng huí jiā kàn wǒ bàba, māma. Xīngqīyī wǎnshang zěnmeyàng?
Gāo Míng:	Wǒ bù xǐhuan wǎnshang dǎ qiú.
Lǐ Dōng:	Nà nǐ wǎnshang dōu zuò shénme?
Gāo Míng:	Wǒ wǎnshang kàn diànshì, shàng wǎng, zuò zuòyè .... Nǐ ne?
Lǐ Dōng:	Xiàtiān wǒ tī zúqiú, dōngtiān wǒ dǎ wǎngqiú.
Gāo Míng:	Nǐ bú zuò zuòyè ma?
Lǐ Dōng:	Zuò, wǒ zǎoshang zuò. Wǒmen de zuòyè hěn shǎo.
Gāo Míng:	Zhè gè xīngqītiān nǐ huí jiā, wǒmen xià gè xīngqītiān qù dǎ wǎngqiú, hǎo bu hǎo?

Lǐ Dōng: Hǎo! Xià gè xīngqītiān jiàn.
Gāo Míng: Xià gè xīngqītiān jiàn.

Reading   Zhōngguó Hé Yīngguó

Zhōngguó shì yí gè dà guó, dì dà rén duō. Yīngguó bǐ Zhōngguó xiǎo, Yīngguó de rénkǒu (population) yě bǐ Zhōngguó shǎo duō le. Dōngtiān, Zhōngguó de běifāng hěn lěng, Běijīng jiù bǐ Lúndūn lěng hěn duō, kěshì nánfāng (south) yǒu de dìfang hé Yīngguó chàbuduō (about the same). Xiàtiān, Zhōngguó bǐ Yīngguó rè, Yīngguó de xiàtiān tiānqì hěn hǎo, bù lěng bú rè. Zhōngguó de chūntiān bǐ Yīnguó nuǎnhuo, Yīngguó de chūntiān hé Zhōngguó de qiūtiān chàbuduō, yǒu yìdiǎnr lěng. Zhōngguó xiàtiān yǔ duō, dōngtiān xuě duō. Yīngguó hěn shǎo xià xuě, chūnxià qiūdōng dōu chángcháng xià yǔ.

Zhōngguórén xǐhuan dǎ yǔmáoqiú, Yīngguórén xǐhuan tī zúqiú. Zhōngguó rén xǐhuan chī mǐfàn (plain rice), Yīngguórén xǐhuan chī chǎofàn. Zhōngguórén xǐhuan hē báijiǔ hé píjiǔ, Yīngguórén xǐhuan hē hóngjiǔ hé píjiǔ. Zhōngguórén xǐhuan gēn péngyou zài jiā (at home) hē jiǔ, Yīngguórén xǐhuan qù jiǔbā (pub) hē jiǔ. Zhōngguórén chángcháng chī hóngshāoròu, Yīngguórén chángcháng chī kǎo niúròu. Zhōngguórén xǐhuan hē lǜchá (green tea), Yīngguórén xǐhuan hē hóngchá (black tea). Zhōngguó qí zìxíngchē de rén duō, Yīngguó kāi chē de rén duō. Kěshì, Zhōngguó hé Yīngguó de qīngniánrén (young people) dōu xǐhuan chī Měiguó (USA) kuàicān (fast food), kàn Měiguó diànyǐng (film).

Lesson 11   Dàyīng Túshūguǎn Zài Nǎr?

Dialogue One
Gāo Míng: Nín hǎo, Zhāng lǎoshī zài ma?
Lǐ Guì: Tā bú zài, tā jīntiān zài Dàyīng Túshūguǎn kàn shū.
Gāo Míng: Qǐng wèn, Dàyīng Túshūguǎn zài nǎr?
Lǐ Guì: Zài huǒchēzhàn de pángbiānr.
Gāo Míng: Nǎ gè huǒchēzhàn?
Lǐ Guì: Guówáng Shízì huǒchēzhàn.
Gāo Míng: Guówáng Shízì huǒchēzhàn zài nǎr?
Lǐ Guì: Zài Yàfēi Xuéyuàn de dōngběibian.
Gāo Míng: Xièxie. Duìbuqǐ, nǎ miàn shì dōng? Nǎ miàn shì xī?
Lǐ Guì: Nǐ zuǒmiàn shì dōng, yòumiàn shì xī.
Gāo Míng: Xièxie. Zàijiàn!

Dialogue Two
Xiǎo Wáng: Dàmíng, Zhōngguó Dàshǐguǎn zài nǎr?
Xiǎo Lǐ: Zài   Yàfēi Xuéyuàn de xīnánmiàn.
Xiǎo Wáng: Dàshǐguǎn nánmiàn shì yí gè dà gōngyuán, duì ba?
Xiǎo Lǐ: Bú duì. Gōngyuán zài dàshǐguǎn de běibian.
Xiǎo Wáng: Dàshǐguǎn wàimiàn yǒu méiyǒu gōnggòng qìchēzhàn?

Xiǎo Lǐ:	Yǒu. Dàshǐguǎn duìmiàn yǒu yí gè yínháng, chēzhàn jiù zài yínháng qiántou.
Xiǎo Wáng:	Yǒu méiyǒu dìtiězhàn?
Xiǎo Lǐ:	Yě yǒu. Dìtiězhàn zài dàshǐguǎn hé gōngyuán de zhōngjiān.
Xiǎo Wáng:	Xièxie. Wǒ míngtiān xiǎng qù dàshǐguǎn, hái xiǎng qù shūdiàn.
Xiǎo Lǐ:	Dàshǐguǎn hòumiàn jiù yǒu yí gè shūdiàn.
Xiǎo Wáng:	Lǐmiàn yǒu Zhōngwénshū ma?
Xiǎo Lǐ:	Yǒu.

Reading   Lúndūn Dàxué Yàfēi Xuéyuàn

Yàfēi Xuéyuàn shì Lúndūn Dàxué de yí gè xuéyuàn. Xuéyuàn bú dà, kěshì hěn yǒumíng (famous). Xuéyuàn yǒu yí gè hěn dà de túshūguǎn, lǐmiàn yǒu hěn duō túshū, yǒu Yīngwén de, Zhōngwén de, hán yǒu Rìwén de děngdeng (etc.). Tiāntiān dōu yǒu hěn duō xuéshēng hé lǎoshī qù túshūguǎn jiè (borrow) shū, huán shū, kàn shū.

Yàfēi Xuéyuàn zài Dàyīng Túshūguǎn de xīnánmiàn, Dàyīng Bówùguǎn (museum) de xīběimiàn. Xuéyuàn de dōngběimiàn yǒu sān gè Zhōngguó fànguǎnr, nàr de Zhōngguófàn hěn hǎochī, yě bú guì, xuéshengmen dōu xǐhuan qù nàr chī fàn. Xuéyuàn de dōngbian shì yí gè xiǎo gōngyuán, xībian shì yí gè hěn dà de shūdiàn. Shūdiàn pángbiān yǒu yí gè jiǔbā. Hěn duō xuéshēng hé lǎoshī xīngqīwǔ wǎnshang dōu qù nàr hē jiǔ.

Lesson 12   Kuàngquánshuǐ Duōshǎo Qián Yì Píng?

Dialogue One

Mǎi Fāng:	Qǐng wèn, kělè duōshao qián yì píng?
Mài Fāng:	Xiǎopíngde sì kuài, dàpíngde bā kuài.
Mǎi Fāng:	Kuàngquánshuǐ ne?
Mài Fāng:	Liǎng kuài qián yì píng.
Mǎi Fāng:	Wǒ mǎi yì píng kuàngquánshuǐ.
Mài Fāng:	Hǎo. Nǐ hái yào diǎnr shénme?
Mǎi Fāng:	Yǒu méiyǒu míngxìnpiàn?
Mài Fāng:	Yǒu, míngxìnpiàn yí kuài liǎng máo wǔ yì zhāng. Nǐ yào jǐ zhāng?
Mǎi Fāng:	Wǒ yào wǔ zhāng. Yígòng duōshao qián?
Mài Fāng:	Yígòng bā kuài liǎng máo wǔ fēn.
Mǎi Fāng:	Zhè shì shí kuài.
Mài Fāng:	Zhǎo nǐ yí kuài qī máo wǔ. Xièxie.

Dialogue Two

Mài Fāng:	Nǐ hǎoí Nǐ xiǎng mǎi diǎnr shénme?
Mǎi Fāng:	Zhè běn xiǎoshuō duōshao qián?
Mài Fāng:	Èrshíwǔ kuài.
Mǎi Fāng:	Guāngpán zěnme mài?
Mài Fāng:	Shí kuài qián yì zhāng.

Mǎi Fāng:	Yǒu méiyǒu Zhōngguó yīnyuè guāngpán?
Mài Fāng:	Yǒu. Zhōngguó yīnyuè, Xīfāng yīnyuè, wǒ zhèr dōu yǒu.
Mǎi Fāng:	Shí kuài tài guì le, néng bu néng piányi diǎnr?
Mài Fāng:	Èrshí zhāng yì bǎi kuài, mǎi yī sòng yī, zěnmeyàng?
Mǎi Fāng:	Èrshí zhāng tài duō le. Wǒ mǎi shí zhāng, wǔshí kuài, xíng bu xíng?
Mài Fāng:	Bù xíng. Wǔshí kuài tài shǎo le, liùshí kuài ba.
Mǎi Fāng:	Hǎo ba, nà jiù liùshí kuài ba.

Reading　　　　　　　　　　Zhōngguórén Mǎi Qìchē

Zài Zhōngguó, yì píng píjiǔ zhǐyào wǔ kuài qián zuǒyòu, yì zhī Běijīng kǎoyā yě zhǐ yào qì-bāshí kuài qián. Zhōngguó chīde, hēde dōu hěn piányi, kěshì yǒude (some) dōngxi (thing) hěn guì, Zhōngguó de fángzi (house) hé qìchē jiù hěn guì.

Zhōngguórén yǐqián (before) qián bù duō, dàjiā (all) dōu qí zìxíngchē. Xiànzài (now) bùshǎo de rén dōu yǒu qìchē, yīnwèi dàjiā dōu bǐ yǐqián yǒu qián. Yǒude rén qián hěn duō, tāmen bù mǎi Zhōngguó chē, tāmen mǎi wàiguó chē. Wàiguó chē bǐ Zhōngguó chē guì duō le. Hái yǒude rén fēicháng (exceptionally) yǒu qián, tāmen bù xǐhuan kāi piányi de wàiguó chē, tāmen xǐ huan kāi wàiguó míngchè (brand name car). Wàiguó míngchè fēicháng guì. Zài Zhōngguó, xiànzài kāi wàiguó míngchè de dàduō (mostly) shì shāngrén hé lǜshī, kāi Zhōngguó chē de dàduō shì yīshēng hé lǎoshī, qí zìxíngchē de dàduō shì gōngrén hé xuésheng.

Lesson 13　　Cāntīng Jǐdiǎn Kāimén?

Dialogue One

Zhāng Liàng:	Qǐng wèn, xiànzài jǐ diǎn?
Lǐ Dàmíng:	Shí diǎn sānshíwǔ fēn. Nǐ shì xīn lái de jiāohuàn xuésheng ba?
Zhāng Liàng:	Duì. Wǒ jiào Zhāng Liàng.
Lǐ Dàmíng:	Wǒ jiào Lǐ Dàmíng.
Zhāng Liàng:	Nǐmen jǐ diǎn kāishǐ shàng kè?
Lǐ Dàmíng:	Jiǔ diǎn.
Zhāng Liàng:	Zhème wǎn! Nǐmen jǐ diǎn chī zǎofàn?
Lǐ Dàmíng:	Bā diǎn zuǒyòu.
Zhāng Liàng:	Xuéxiào lǐmiàn yǒu méiyǒu cāntīng?
Lǐ Dàmíng:	Yǒu. Cāntīng zǎoshang bù kāimén. Shàngwǔ chà yí kè shíyī diǎn kāimén.
Zhāng Liàng:	Jǐ diǎn guānmén?
Lǐ Dàmíng:	Wǎnshang liù diǎn.
Zhāng Liàng:	Túshūguǎn jǐ diǎn kāimén?
Lǐ Dàmíng:	Túshūguǎn shàngwǔ bā diǎn bàn kāimén, wǎnshang shí diǎn bàn guānmén.
Zhāng Liàng:	Xièxie.

Dialogue Two

Zhāng Liàng:	Nǐ hǎo, wǒ shì xīn lái de jiāohuàn xuésheng. Xuéxiào fùjìn yǒu shuǐguǒdiàn ma?

Wáng Jīng: Yǒu, xuéxiào dōngmiàn jiù yǒu yì jiā.
Zhāng Liàng: Shuǐguǒdiàn shénme shíhou guānmén?
Wáng Jīng: Shuǐguǒdiàn èrshísì xiǎoshí dōu kāi, bù guānmén.
Zhāng Liàng: Tài hǎo le, xièxie. Zhèr de shuǐguǒ guì bu guì?
Wáng Jīng: Bú guì. Píngguǒ yì jīn sì kuài qián zuǒyòu.
Zhāng Liàng: Yǒu méiyǒu Yīngguó píngguǒ?
Wáng Jīng: Méiyǒu. Yǒu Rìběn píngguǒ.
Zhāng Liàng: Rìběn píngguǒ duōshao qián yì jīn?
Wáng Jīng: Rìběn píngguǒ chàbuduō shí kuài qián yì jīn.

Reading   Túshūguǎn Kāifàng (open) Shíjiān (time)

Dōngnán Dàxué shì yí gè hěn dà de dàxué, yǒu shí gè xuéyuàn. Xuéxiào yǒu dōng, xī liǎng gè xiàoyuán (campus), dōng xiàoyuán shì lǎo (old) xiàoyuán, xī xiàoyuán shì xīn xiàoyuán. Liǎng gè xiàoyuán dōu yǒu túshūguǎn. Yīxué, shāngxué, wénxué, yǔyánxué de shū dōu zài dōng xiàoyuán túshūguǎn, qítā (other) de shū dōu zài xī xiàoyuán de xīn túshūguǎn. Xiàmiàn shì liǎng gè túshūguǎn de kāifàng shíjiān.

Lesson 14   Zǒulù Qù Yīyuàn Yào Jǐ Fēnzhōng?

Dialogue One
Wènlùrén: Qǐng wèn, qù Dì-yī Yīyuàn zěnme zǒu?
Lùrén: Nǐ yìzhí xiàng qián zǒu, dào hónglǜdēng xiàng yòu guǎi.
Wènlùrén: Ránhòu ne?
Lùrén: Zǒu dào dì-sān gè shízì lùkǒu zài xiàng zuǒ guǎi, zuǒbian jiù shì Dì-yī Yīyuàn.
Wènlùrén: Xièxie. Zǒulù yào jǐ fēnzhōng?
Lùrén: Yào èrshí fēnzhōng zuǒyòu.
Wènlùrén: Yǒu gōnggòng qìchē ma?
Lùrén: Yǒu. Kěyǐ zuò sān èr wǔ lù qù.
Wènlùrén: Zuò chē yào jǐ fēnzhōng?
Lùrén: Zuò chē zhǐyào wǔ fēnzhōng.
Wènlùrén: Yígòng yào zuò jǐ zhàn?
Lùrén: Sì zhàn.
Wènlùrén: Xièxie.

Dialogue Two
Yīshēng: Wáng xiǎojiě, nǐ nǎr bù shūfu?
Wáng Xiǎoyīng: Wǒ tóu téng.
Yīshēng: Fāshāo ma?
Wáng Xiǎoyīng: Bù fāshāo.
Yīshēng: Wǒ kànkan. Nǐ yǒudiǎnr gǎnmào. Dǎ yì zhēn ba.
Wáng Xiǎoyīng: Yīshēng, wǒ bù xiǎng dǎ zhēn, chī yào kěyǐ ma?
Yīshēng: Nǐ xiǎng chī zhōngyào háishi chī xīyào?

Wáng Xiǎoyīng:	Wǒ xiǎng chī xīyào.
Yīshēng:	Hǎo, zhè shì nǐ de yàofāng. Nǐ yào hǎohāo xiūxi, duō hē kāishuǐ.
Wáng Xiǎoyīng:	Xièxie. Zhè yào zěnme chī?
Yīshēng:	Yí rì sān cì, yí cì liǎng piàn, fàn hòu chī.
Wáng Xiǎoyīng:	Duìbuqǐ, fùjìn yǒu yàodiàn ma?
Yīshēng:	Yǒu, duìmiàn jiù yǒu yí gè.

Reading   "Zhōngguó Rénmín Hěn Xíng"

Wǒ bàba zài Běijīng gōngzuò, qùnián wǒ qù Běijīng kàn tā. Yǒu yì tiān, wǒ yǒudiǎnr gǎnmào, xiǎng qù yàodiàn mǎi diǎnr yào. Kěshì wǒ bàba nà tiān hěn máng, bù néng hé wǒ yìqǐ qù. Yīnwèi wǒ huì shuō yìdiǎn Hànyǔ, rènshi jǐ gè Hànzì, suǒyǐ (therefore) wǒ shuō wǒ yí gè rén qù, wǒ néng zhǎodào yàodiàn.

Wǒ bàba shuō wǒmen jiā fùjìn jiù yǒu yí gè xiǎo yàodiàn. Tā shuō wǒ zài dì-yī gè shízì lùkǒu xiàng yòu guǎi, ránhòu dào dì-èr gè shízì lùkǒu xiàng zuǒ guǎi, zǒu wǔ fēnzhōng, zuǒbian jiù shì Zhōngguó Rénmín Yínháng, xiǎo yàodiàn jiù zài yínháng de pángbiān. Tā hái shuō, "Yàoshi (if) nǐ bú rènshi lù, wènwen Zhōngguórén, tāmen dōu hěn xǐhuan bāngzhù (help) rén. "

Wǒ xiǎng zhǐyào (so long as) zhǎodào (find) Zhōngguó Rénmín Yínháng, jiù kěyǐ zhǎodào yàodiàn. Kěshì wǒ zhǎole (looked for) bàn gè xiǎoshí, zhǐ kànjiàn (see) yí gè "Zhōngguó Rénmín Hěn Xíng". Wǒ zhǐhǎo (have to) wèn yí gè xiǎo péngyou qù yínháng zěnme zǒu. Xiǎo péngyou shuō, "zhè bú jiù shì yínháng de dàmén ma?" Yuánlái (it turns out) "Zhōngguó Rénmín Hěn Xíng" jiù shì "Zhōngguó Rénmín Yínháng".

Lesson 15   Yīngbàng Shàngzhǎng Le!

Dialogue One

Lǐ Dōng:	Xiǎo Wáng, shàng xīngqīwǔ nǐ zěnme méi lái shàng kè?
Wáng Jīng:	Wǒ qù kàn bìng le. Wǒ gǎnmào le.
Lǐ Dōng:	Nǐ chī yào le ma?
Wáng Jīng:	Chī le.
Lǐ Dōng:	Xiànzài tiānqì lěng le, gǎnmào de rén yě duō le.
Wáng Jīng:	Qù yīyuàn kàn bìng de rén yě duō le.
Lǐ Dōng:	Nǐ děi duō xiūxi liǎng tiān.
Wáng Jīng:	Wǒ xiànzài yǐjīng hǎo le. Xiǎo Lǐ, nǐ bǐ yǐqián shòu le?
Lǐ Dōng:	Wǒ shì shòule yìdiǎnr. Wǒ yǐqián tài pàng le.
Wáng Jīng:	Nǐ xiànzài duōshao gōngjīn?
Lǐ Dōng:	Liùshíwǔ gōngjīn, bǐ yǐqián shòule wǔ gōngjīn.
Wáng Jīng:	Wǒ xiànzài hěn shǎo qù dǎ wǎngqiú, nǐ hái tiāntiān qù dǎ ma?
Lǐ Dōng:	Wǒ xiànzài bù dǎ wǎngqiú le, wǒ dǎ tàijíquán le.

Dialogue Two

Wáng Xiǎoyīng:	Qǐng wèn, yì bǎi měiyuán huàn duōshao rénmínbì?
Lǐ Xiānsheng:	Liù bǎi sānshí kuài.
Wáng Xiǎoyīng:	Bú shì néng huàn liù bǎi sānshí qī kuài ma?
Lǐ Xiānsheng:	Zuótiān néng huàn nàme duō, jīntiān měiyuán xiàdiē le.
Wáng Xiǎoyīng:	Yì bǎi yīngbàng néng huàn duōshao Rénmínbì?
Lǐ Xiānsheng:	Jiǔ bǎi jiǔshí jiǔ kuài. Yīngbàng shàngzhǎng le. Ōuyuán yě shàngzhǎng le.
Wáng Xiǎoyīng:	Yì bǎi ōuyuán néng huàn duōshao kuài?
Lǐ Xiānsheng:	Bā bǎi sìshí qī kuài.
Wáng Xiǎoyīng:	Wǒ huàn wǔ bǎi ōuyuán. Nǐmen shōu bu shōu lǚxíng zhīpiào?
Lǐ Xiānsheng:	Shōu, wǒmen jì shōu lǚxíng zhīpiào, yě shōu xiànjīn.

Reading   Wáng Xiānsheng Shénme Shíhou Néng Qù Zhōngguó?

Wáng xiānsheng yìzhí (all the time) xiǎng qù Zhōngguó kànkan, kěshì tā méiyǒu hěn duō qián, suǒyǐ qián jǐ nián, tā chàbuduō tiāntiān dōu qù yínháng kàn huìlǜ, xīwàng (hope) yīngbàng shàngzhǎng. Kěshì huìlǜ tiāntiān dōu bù yíyàng, jīntiān yīngbàng shàngzhǎng le, míngtiān rénmínbì shàngzhǎng le, hòutiān yīngbàng xiàdiē le, dàhòutiān měiyuán xiàdiē le. Suǒyǐ Wáng xiānsheng yìzhí méiyǒu qù Zhōngguó.

Zuótiān, wǒ zài jiǔbā li kànjiàn tā le. Tā duì (to) wǒ shuō tā xiànzài bú qù Zhōngguó le. Wǒ wèn tā wèishénme bú qù le, tā shuō xiànzài rénmínbì shàngzhǎng le, qù Zhōngguó tài guì le, tā yào qù Měiguó, yīnwèi měiyuán xiàdiē le. Wǒ shuō rénmínbì hái yào shàngzhǎng, xiànzài jiù yīnggāi qù Zhōngguó. Wáng Xiānsheng shuō, "Wǒ děng (wait) xiàdiē le zài qù." Wǒ duì tā shuō, "Nǐ bú yào (do not) děng le, yīnwèi nǐ kěnéng yào děng hěn cháng (long) shíjiān."

Lesson 16   Wǒ Shì Zuò Gōnggòng Qìchē Lái De

Dialogue One

Wáng Jīng:	Duìbuqǐ, wǒ lái wǎn le. Ràng nǐ jiǔ děng le.
Lǐ Xiǎoyīng:	Méi guānxi. Wǒ yě shì gāng dào.
Wáng Jīng:	Jīntiān dìtiě huài le, nǐ shì zěnme lái de?
Lǐ Xiǎoyīng:	Wǒ shì zuò gōnggòng qìchē lái de.
Wáng Jīng:	Nǐ huāle duō cháng shíjiān?
Lǐ Xiǎoyīng:	Wǒ huāle yí gè duō xiǎoshí. Nǐ shì zěnme lái de?
Wáng Jīng:	Wǒ shì zuò chūzūchē lái de.
Lǐ Xiǎoyīng:	Zuò chūzūchē yídìng hěn guì. Nǐ jiā lí xuéxiào yuǎn bu yuǎn?
Wáng Jīng:	Wǒ jiā lí xuéxiào hěn jìn, wǒ zhǐ huāle bā bàng qián.
Lǐ Xiǎoyīng:	Nǐ tōngcháng zěnme lái xuéxiào?
Wáng Jīng:	Wǒ hěn shǎo zuò chūzūchē. Yǒushíhou qí chē, yǒushíhou zǒu lù.

Dialogue Two

Wáng Jīng:	Xiǎo Lǐ, nǐ zuótiān qù méi qù kàn zúqiú bǐsài?

Lǐ Dōng:　　　Qù le. Búguò wǒ zhǐ kànle shàngbànchǎng.
Wáng Jīng:　　Nǐ bú shì hěn ài kàn zúqiú bǐsài ma?
Lǐ Dōng:　　　Zuótiān wǒ shì hé wǒ nǚpéngyou yìqǐ qù de, tā kànle yíbàn jiù bù xiǎng kàn le.
Wáng Jīng:　　Wǒ yǐqián yě zǒngshì hé wǒ nǚpéngyou yìqǐ qù kàn.
Lǐ Dōng:　　　Xiànzài ne?
Wáng Jīng:　　Wǒ xiànzài méiyǒu nǚpéngyou le.
Lǐ Dōng:　　　Zhēn de? Shì bu shì yīnwèi nǐ tài ài kàn zúqiú le, suǒyǐ tā líkāi nǐ le?
Wáng Jīng:　　Duì. Tā shuō wǒ bù xūyào nǚpéngyou, zúqiú jiù shì wǒ de nǚpéngyou.
Lǐ Dōng:　　　Kànlái yǐhòu wǒ yě bù néng cháng qù kàn zúqiúsài le.

Reading　　　　　　　　　　Wǒmen Shì Zài Fǎguó Rènshi De

Qùnián de xīnnián wǒ shì zài Fǎguó guò (pass) de. Wǒ qù Fǎguó kàn wǒ nǎinai (grandma). Wǒ shì zuò fēijī qù de. Xiàle fēijī yǐhòu, wǒ qù zhǎo xíngli (luggage) chē, yí wèi fēicháng piàoliang de nǚhái (girl) yě zài zhǎo. Wǒ méiyǒu hé tā shuō huà.

Dì-èr tiān, wǒ hé wǒ nǎinai qù shāngdiàn mǎi dōngxi (shopping), wǒ yòu (again) kànjiànle nà gè nǚhái. Tā yě kànjiànle wǒ. Wǒ wèn tā shì nǎ guó rén, tā shuō tā shì Yīngguórén. Wǒ yòu wèn tā shì shénme dìfang rén, tā shuō tā shì Lúndūnrén. Wǒ shuō wǒ yě shì Lúndūnrén, wǒ zài Běi Lúndūn Gōngxuéyuàn (polytechnic) shàng xué. Tā shuō tā yě shì Běi Lúndūn Gōngxuéyuàn de xuésheng, tā jiā lí xuéyuàn hěn jìn, jiù zài xuéyuàn pángbiān. Wǒmen liǎng gè dōu shì Yīngguórén, dōu zài yí gè xuéxiào li shàng xué, kěshì tā bú rènshi wǒ, wǒ yě bú rènshi tā. Wǒmen shì zài Fǎguó rènshi de. Xiànzài tā shì wǒ de nǚpéngyou.

Lesson 17　　　Nǐ Pǔtōnghuà Shuō De Hěn Liúlì

Dialogue One
Wáng Jing:　　Nǐ hǎo, kěyǐ qǐng nǐ tiào wǔ ma?
Lǐ Hóng:　　　Ā, nǐ huì shuō pǔtōnghuài
Wáng Jing:　　Wǒ shuō de bú tài liúlì.
Lǐ Hóng:　　　Nǐ shuō de hěn búcuò. Nǐ xuéle duō cháng shíjiān de Zhōngwén?
Wáng Jing:　　Wǒ xuéle bàn nián le.
Lǐ Hóng:　　　Xuéle bàn nián jiù shuō de zhème hǎo. Zhēn bù róngyì! Nǐ shì zài nǎr xué de?
Wáng Jing:　　Duìbuqǐ, nǐ shuō de tài kuài le, qǐng nǐ zài shuō yí biàn.
Lǐ Hóng:　　　Wǒ shuō nǐ de Zhōngwén shuō de hěn hǎo, nǐ shì zài nǎr xué de?
Wáng Jing:　　Wǒ shì zài Lúndūn Dàxué xué de.
Lǐ Hóng:　　　Nǐ xuéle jǐ běn Zhōngwén shū le?
Wáng Jing:　　Wǒ cái xuéle yì běn. Búguò wǒ nǚpéngyou shì Shànghǎirén.
Lǐ Hóng:　　　Guàibude nǐ Zhōngwén shuō de zhème hǎo!

Dialogue Two
Wáng Jīng:　　Xiǎo Lǐ, zuótiān wǎnshang de wǎnhuì kāi de zěnmeyàng?
Lǐ Xiǎoyīng:　Kāi de hěn chénggōng. Dàmíng hái chàngle yí gè Zhōngguó gēr.

Wáng Jīng:	Zhēn de? Tā chàng de hǎo bu hǎo?
Lǐ Xiǎoyīng:	Tā chàng de hǎo jí le. Fāng Yīng wǔ tiào de yě hěn hǎo.
Wáng Jīng:	Nǐ tiào wǔ tiào de yě búcuò, nǐ tiàole méiyǒu?
Lǐ Xiǎoyīng:	Méiyǒu. Wǒ tiào de bù zěnmeyàng. Wǒ biǎoyǎnle Zhōngguó gōngfu.
Wáng Jīng:	Wǒ cónglái bù zhīdào nǐ huì Zhōngguó gōngfu. Nǐ shì shénme shíhou kāishǐ xué de?
Lǐ Xiǎoyīng:	Wǒ bàn nián yǐqián jiù kāishǐ xué le.
Wáng Jīng:	Nǐ shì gēn shuí xué de?
Lǐ Xiǎoyīng:	Wǒ shì gēn Zhāng Liàng xué de.
Wáng Jīng:	Zhāng Liàng? Tā nàme shòu hái huì Zhōngguó gōngfu?
Lǐ Xiǎoyīng:	Nǐ bú xìn? Tā yí gè rén néng dǎ shí gè rén.
Wáng Jīng:	Zhēn de? Wǒ zǎo jiù xiǎng xué Zhōngguó gōngfu le, wǒ xiànzài jiù qù zhǎo tā, huítóu jiàn.

Reading   Lǐ Dàmíng Pǔtōnghuà Shuō De Zhēn Hǎo

Lǐ Dàmíng shì Yīngguó Lúndūnrén, kěshì tā pǔtōnghuà shuō de hěn hǎo. Yí gè Yīngguórén pǔtōnghuà zěnme shuō de zhème hǎo? Tā shì zěnme xué de ne?

Yuánlái, qiánnián xiàtiān Lǐ Dàmíng hé péngyou yìqǐ qù Zhōngguó wánr (on holiday). Nà shíhou tā de Hànyǔ bù zěnmeyàng. Zài yí gè fànguǎn li, tā shuō yào chī yú (fish), kěshì fúwùyuán (waiter) gěile tā yì pán jī (chicken). Tāmen yīnggāi shí hào líkāi fàndiàn, kěshì fàndiàn yào tāmen sì hào jiù líkāi. Tā hěn shēngqì, kěshì zhè dōu shì yīnwèi tā fā yīn (pronounce) fā de bù hǎo.

Huídào Yīngguó yǐhòu, tā kāishǐ rènzhēn (seriously) xuéxí Zhōngwén. Xiànzài qù Zōngguó fànguǎn diǎn cài zài yě bú huì cuò le. Dàmíng xiànzài yǒu nǔpéngyou le, tā shì Xiānggǎng (Hong Kong) rén, kěshì tā de Pǔtōnghuà hái méiyǒu Dàmíng shuō de hǎo.

Lesson 18   Nǐ Zài Gàn Shénme Ne?

Dialogue One

Lǐ Dōng:	Xiǎo Wáng, nǐ zài gàn shénme ne?
Wáng Jīng:	Wǒ zài zuò liànxí.
Lǐ Dōng:	Zuótiān wǎnshang jiǔ diǎn zuǒyòu nǐ zài gàn shénme?
Wáng Jīng:	Wǒ zài shàng wǎng.
Lǐ Dōng:	Wǒ gěi nǐ dǎ diànhuà, kěshì méi rén jiē. Wǒ hái yǐwéi nǐ shuìjiào le.
Wáng Jīng:	Nǐ zhǎo wǒ yǒu shì ma?
Lǐ Dōng:	Wǒ zhèngzài yòng Zhōngwén xiě xìn, nǐ néng bu néng bāngbang wǒ?
Wáng Jīng:	Nǐ gěi shuí xiě xìn?
Lǐ Dōng:	Wǒ de yí gè Zhōngguó péngyou.
Wáng Jīng:	Shì nǔpéngyou ba? Nǐ ràng wǒ bāng nǐ xiě qíngshū, duì bu duì?
Lǐ Dōng:	Bù, bú shì qíngshū, wǒmen cái gānggāng rènshi.
Wáng Jīng:	Hǎo ba, wǒ bāng nǐ xiě. Nǐmen shì zěnme rènshi de?
Lǐ Dōng:	Wǒ qù Zhōngguó fànguǎnr chī fàn, tā zài nàr dǎ gōng.

Wáng Jīng:	Tā yě shì xuésheng ma?
Lǐ Dōng:	Duì, tā yìbiānr shàng xué, yìbiānr dǎ gōng.

Dialogue Two

Zhāng Liàng:	Wǒmen zhèng shuō nǐ ne, nǐ jiù lái le.
Lǐ Dōng:	Nǐmen zài shuō wǒ shénme?
Zhāng Liàng:	Wǒmen zài shuō bù zhīdào nǐ zuìjìn zài máng shénme.
Lǐ Dōng:	Wǒ zhèngzài zhǔnbèi kǎo shì.
Xiè Hóng:	Nǐ shénme shíhou kǎo?
Lǐ Dōng:	Xià xīngqī jiù kǎo. Xīngqīyī kǎo kǒushì, xīngqī'èr kǎo bǐshì. Duì le, Xiǎo Zhāng, wǒ zhèng xiǎng jiè nǐ de Hàn-Yīng zìdiǎn yòng yíxià.
Zhāng Liàng:	Méi wèntí. Nǐ shénme shíhou yòng?
Lǐ Dōng:	Xià xīngqī'èr, kǎo bǐshì de shíhou yòng.
Xiè Hóng:	Nǐ de diànzǐ zìdiǎn bù néng yòng ma?
Lǐ Dōng:	Zhāng lǎoshī shuō kǎoshì de shíhou bù néng yòng.
Xiè Hóng:	Jǐ diǎn le? Wǒ yī diǎnzhōng yào qù jiàn Zhāng lǎoshī.
Zhāng Liàng:	Xiànzài yǐjīng yī diǎn le. Kuài qù ba, tā yídìng zhèngzài děng nǐ ne.

Reading   Xiǎo Lǐ "Zuò Kè" (be a guest)

Xiǎo Lǐ hé tā nǚpéngyou Xiǎo Fāng yǐjīng rènshi bàn nián duō le. Yǒu yì tiān, Xiǎo Fāng duì tā shuō, "Wǒ bàba māma xiǎng jiànjian nǐ, nǐ xīngqīliù zhōngwǔ lái wǒ jiā chī fàn ba."

Xiǎo Lǐ tīngle fēicháng gāoxìng (happy). Xīngqīliù shàngwǔ tā xiān qù shāngchǎng mǎile liǎng gè lǐwù (gift), bú dào shí'èr diǎn tā jiù zuò chūzūchē qù Xiǎo Fāng jiā le. Xīngqīliù lùshang chē hěn duō, tōngcháng dào Xiǎo Fāng jiā zhǐ xūyào shí fēnzhōng, kěshì nà tiān huāle bàn gè duō xiǎoshí. Dào Xiǎo Fāng jiā de shíhou yǐjīng shí'èr diǎn bàn le. Xiǎo Fāng duì Xiǎo Lǐ shuō, "Nǐ zěnme cái lái? Wǒmen dōu zài děng nǐ ne." Xiǎo Lǐ yǐwéi tāmen zài děng tā chī fàn, kěshì Xiǎo Fāng de māma shuō, "Wǒmen dōu bú è, nǐ mànmān (slowly) zuò ba." Xiǎo Fāng de bàba shuō, "Wǒ zhèli yǒu píjiǔ. Nǐ kěyǐ yìbiān zuò fàn, yìbiān hē píjiǔ." Yuánlái Xiǎo Fāng shuō tā fàn zuò de fēicháng hǎochī, dàjiā zhèngzài děng tā lái zuò fàn ne.

Lesson19   Wǒ Gāng Mǎi De Diànnǎo Yòu Piányi Yòu Hǎo

Dialogue One

Wáng Jīng:	Xiǎo Lǐ, zhè jiù shì nǐ zuótiān gāng mǎi de diànnǎo ma?
Lǐ Dōng:	Duì. Zhè tái diànnǎo bǐ wǒ qùnián mǎi de nà tái kuài duō le.
Wáng Jīng:	Nǐ shì zài nǎr mǎi de?
Lǐ Dōng:	Zài xuéxiào pángbiān nà jiā xīn kāi de shāngdiàn li mǎi de.
Wáng Jīng:	Nàr mài bu mài shǒutí diànnǎo? Wǒ xiǎng gěi wǒ nǚpéngyou mǎi yí gè.
Lǐ Dōng:	Mài. Nàli yǒu gèzhǒng páizi de shǒutí diànnǎo.
Wáng Jīng:	Yǒu méiyǒu jìnkǒu de?
Lǐ Dōng:	Yǒu. Yǒu Měiguó de, Rìběn de ...

Wáng Jīng: Yǒu méiyǒu Zhōngguó shēngchǎn de?
Lǐ Dōng: Yǒu. Nǐ wèishénme duì Zhōngguó shēngchǎn de diànnǎo gǎn xìngqù?
Wáng Jīng: Yīnwèi wǒ nǚpéngyou xǐhuan. Tā shuō Zhōngguó zhìzào de dōngxi yòu piányi
              yòu hǎo.

Dialogue Two
Wáng Jīng: Lǐ Dōng, zuótiān lái zhǎo nǐ de nà gè nǚhái shì shuí?
Lǐ Dōng: Shì wǒ mèimei.
Wáng Jīng: Wǒ hái yǐwéi shì nǐ gāng rènshi de nǚpéngyou ne.
Lǐ Dōng: Zuótiān shàng kè shí dǎ diànhuà gěi wǒ de cái shì wǒ nǚpényou.
Wáng Jīng: Dāngshí dàjiā dōu zài rènzhēn tīng kè, lǎoshī hěn bù gāoxìng.
Lǐ Dōng: Wǒ zhīdào, wǒ wàngle guān jī le.
Wáng Jīng: Nǐ yòng de shì shénme shǒujī? Wǒ zhè gè shì qùnián gāng mǎi de, yǐjīng guòshí
              le.
Lǐ Dōng: Wǒ de shì zuìxīn chǎnpǐn. Nǐ kànkan.
Wáng Jīng: Zhēn piàoliang!
Lǐ Dōng: Piàoliang shì piàoliang, jiù shì tài guì le.
Wáng Jīng: Nǐ shì huā duōshao qián mǎi de?
Lǐ Dōng: Zhè bú shì wǒ mǎi de, shì wǒ nǚpéngyou sònggěi wǒ de shēngri lǐwù.

Reading   Lúndūn De Zhōngwén Shūdiàn

Lúndūn yǒu hěn duō mài Zhōngwén shū de shūdiàn. Yàoshi nǐ xiǎng mǎi Zhōngwén shū,
kěyǐ qù Zhōngguó Chéng (Chinatown) mǎi, nàli yǒu liǎng-sān jiā Zhōngwén shūdiàn. Nǐ yě
kěyǐ qù pǔtōng dà shūdiàn mǎi, xiànzài hěn duō Yīngguó shūdiàn dōu kāishǐ mài Zhōngwén
shū le. Búguò, Lúndūn hái yǒu yì jiā zhuānmén (specialised) mài Zhōngwén túshū de gōngsī
(company). Zhè jiā gōngsī hěn dà, lǐmiàn yǒu hěn duō Zhōngwén shū hé Zhōngwén guāngpán.

Zhè jiā gōngsī shì Zhōngguó Túshū Zǒng Gōngsī (parent company) de Lúndūn fēn gōngsī
(subsidiary). Gōngsī lí dìtiězhàn hé gōnggòng qìchēzhàn dōu bù yuǎn. Gōngsī li de Zhōngwén
shū yǒu Hànyǔ kǒuyǔ, Hànyǔ xiězuò, Hànyǔ yǔfǎ, Zhōngguó wénxué hé shūfǎ děngděng.
Zhèxiē shū dàduō shì Běijīng Dàxué, Běijīng Yǔyán Dàxué de lǎoshī xiě de. Gōngsī hái yǒu
hěn duō Zhōngguó yīnyuè hé Zhōngguó diànyǐng guāngpán. Yǒu shíjiān nǐ kěyǐ qù kànkan,
yídìng néng mǎidào nǐ xǐhuan de dōngxi.

Lessons 20   Nǐ Qùguò Chángchéng Ma?

Dialogue One
Xiǎo Lǐ: Xiǎo Huáng, mǎshàng jiù yào fàng jià le, nǐ dǎsuan qù nǎr wánr?
Xiǎo Huáng: Wǒ dǎsuan qù Zhōnguó de Hǎinán. Tīngshuō nàli měi jí le.
Xiǎo Lǐ: Měi shì měi, jiù shì tài yuǎn le.
Xiǎo Huáng: Nǐ dǎsuan qù nǎr dù jià?
Xiǎo Lǐ: Qù Ōuzhōu dàlù.

Xiǎo Huáng: Nǐ cónglái méiyǒu qùguo Ōuzhōu dàlù ma?

Xiǎo Lǐ: Qù shì qùguo, kěshì méiyǒu hǎohāo wánrguo.

Xiǎo Huáng: Zhè cì nǐ dǎsuan qù nǎxiē guójiā?

Xiǎo Lǐ: Wǒ xiǎng xiān qù Bǐlìshí, qùle Bǐlìshí qù Déguó.

Xiǎo Huáng: Qùle Déguó qù Yìdàlì?

Xiǎo Lǐ: Wǒ yǐqián qùguo Yìdàlì le, zhè cì qùle Déguó qù Xībānyá.

Dialogue Two

Xiǎo Lǐ: Xiǎo Wáng, tīngshuō nǐ yào qù Zhōngguó.

Xiǎo Wáng: Duì, wǒ yǐqián cónglái méi qùguo. Nǐ qùguo méiyǒu?

Xiǎo Lǐ: Qùguo hǎo duō cì le.

Xiǎo Wáng: Chángchéng, Chángjiāng nǐ qùguo méiyǒu?

Xiǎo Lǐ: Qùguo.

Xiǎo Wáng: Huángshān, Huánghé nǐ yě qùguo le ma?

Xiǎo Lǐ: Dāngrán qùguo le. Zhōngguó yǒumíng de dìfang wǒ chàbuduō dōu qùguo le.

Xiǎo Wáng: Tīngshuō Yúnnán hěn měi.

Xiǎo Lǐ: Qùguo de rén dōu shuō hěn měi.

Xiǎo Wáng: Zhè cì wǒ xiǎng xiān qù Yúnnán, qùle Yúnnán zài qù Sìchuān kàn dà xióngmāo.

Xiǎo Lǐ: Dà xióngmāo kě'ài jí le. Nǐ méi jiànguo dà xióngmāo ma?

Xiǎo Wáng: Wǒ zhǐ zài dòngwùyuán li jiànguo.

Xiǎo Lǐ: Nǐ dǎsuan shénme shíhou zǒu?

Xiǎo Wáng: Fēijīpiào wǒ dōu mǎi le, yí fàng jià wǒ jiù zǒu.

Reading   Wǒ De Dì-yī Cì Zhōngguó Lǚxíng

Qùguo Zhōngguó de rén dōu zhīdào Zhōngguó hěn dà, hǎo wánr de dìfang yě hěn duō. Wǒ cóng xiǎo jiù duì Zhōngguó gǎn xìngqù, kěshì yìzhí méiyǒu jīhuì (chance) qù. Qùnián xiàtiān jīhuì lái le, wǒ de hǎo péngyou Mǎkè (Mark) nàshí (at that time) zhèngzài Zhōngguó xuéxí Hànyǔ, tā qǐng wǒ qù Zhōngguó dù jià, wǒ gāoxìng jí le. Zhè shì wǒ dì-yī cì qù Zhōngguó.

Wǒ shì xiān dào de Běijīng. Mǎkè nàshí hái méiyǒu fàng jià, wǒ jiù yí gè rén xiān qù kànle Chángchéng. Chángchéng yòu gāo yòu cháng, fēicháng piàoliang. Xuéxiào yí fàng jià, Mǎkè hé wǒ jiù qùle Xī'ān. Wǒmen qùle Xī'ān qù Shāndōng, qùle Shāndōng qù Shànghǎi, qùle Shànghǎi yòu qù Huángshān. Qīyuè de Zhōngguó, tiānqì hěn rè, suīrán Huángshān hěn měi, kěshì wǒmen méiyǒu hǎohāo kàn. Cóng Huángshān yí xiàlái, wǒmen jiù qùle Hǎinán. Hǎinán zhēn shì piàoliang jí le. Wǒmen wánr de fēicháng gāoxìng. Wǒ duì Mǎkè shuō, zhè cì méiyǒu hǎohāo kàn Huángshān, míngnián wǒ yídìng zài lái.

作者简介　About the Authors

Dr George X Zhang is the Director of the Language Centre and London Confucius Institute at the School of Oriental and African Studies, University of London. He has over twenty-five years of experience working in British and Chinese universities with research interests and publications in language acquisition, cross cultural communications and teacher training. He was given a full professorship by the Shandong Normal University in 1994, made an honorary fellow by the Chartered Institute of Linguists in 2010, and is currently the coordinator of the European Benchmarking Chinese Language (EBCL) project.

Linda M Li is the principal lecturer in Chinese and the Deputy Head of the Department of Languages and Cross cultural Studies at Regents College, London. Linda has taught English and Chinese for over twenty years in secondary, tertiary and higher education institutions in China and the UK and has research interests in applied linguistics, social linguistics and language teaching for business purposes. She has also been actively involved in teacher education for the last five years.

Lik Suen is a senior lector of Chinese in the Department of China and Inner Asia at the School of Oriental and African Studies. She is a graduate of the Beijing Language Institute (now the Beijing Language and Culture University) with nearly 15 years' experience of teaching Chinese as a foreign language at universities in China's mainland, Hong Kong and London. She is studying for a PhD in applied linguistics at the University of London.